LEARNING TO SPEAK:
A Manual For Parents

LEARNING TO SPEAK:
A Manual For Parents

Philip R. Zelazo
Montreal Children's Hospital and
McGill University
Richard B. Kearsley
Tufts University School of Medicine
Judy A. Ungerer
Macquarie University
Australia

Ψ Psychology Press
Taylor & Francis Group

New York London

First Published by
Lawrence Erlbaum Associates, Inc., Publishers
365 Broadway
Hillsdale, New Jersey 07642

Transferred to Digital Printing 2009 by Psychology Press
270 Madison Ave, New York NY 10016
27 Church Road, Hove, East Sussex, BN3 2FA

Photos throughout volume by Diane Lizza

Library of Congress Cataloging in Publication Data

Zelazo, Philip R.
Learning to speak.

Bibliography: p.
Includes index.
1. Mentally handicapped children—Education—Language
arts—Handbooks, manuals, etc. 2. Children—Language—
Handbooks, manuals, etc. 3. Domestic education—
United States—Handbooks, manuals, etc. I. Kearsley,
Richard B. II. Ungerer, Judy. III. Title.
LC4616.Z44   1984   649'.68   83-20731
ISBN 0-8058-5945-4
ISBN 0-8058-5946-2

Contents

3. REVERSING NONCOMPLIANT BEHAVIORS

4. AN OVERVIEW OF THE LANGUAGE TEACHING SESSIONS

5. TEACHING SINGLE WORDS

Preface

The reissue of this manual is timely for two reasons: The dramatic increase in the incidence of autism and the use of this program with children who have autism and their parents since 1984 by one of the authors (PRZ). In fact, the original sample of 44 children for whom the manual was written, has been re-evaluated using the Diagnostic and Statistical Manual (4th edition, 1994) and all but one child met the expanded criteria for autism. This manual has been used successfully to produce spontaneous three-word sentences in the majority of children in the original Boston sample (i.e., those with normal information processing ability), in clinical cases seen subsequently at the Montreal Children's Hospital until May 2002, and those treated at the Montreal Autism Centre currently. In all these cases, the manual has been used under the guidance of a professional who was skilled with these procedures, originally the three authors, two psychologists and a behavioral pediatrician/psychologist (RBK).

The three authors used biweekly telephone meetings with half of the original sample of children with normal information processing ability (the other half received office visits instead) and PRZ used telephone conferencing with three additional families and videoconferencing with 12 families subsequently. Nearly all children in the samples acquired spontaneously produced three-word sentences. In Montreal, a total of seven graduate students and clinical psychology staff used the procedures successfully with families and approximately 12 advanced undergraduate students used them in a group setting under close supervision. Some parents have applied the procedures without professional involvement but, we cannot attest to their success because the information was not shared.

Clearly, the guidance of a trained professional, a child psychologist or psychiatrist, speech pathologist, behavioral pediatrician, applied developmental psychologist, or an applied behavior analyst specifically trained with these procedures is most desirable. A trained professional can assist treatment by solving problems that the child may present, setting the next appropriate target as quickly as possible, and motivating parents to continue to the next level of achievement. Clinical experience suggests that the involvement of a trained professional can save time and make the task easier. One benefit of this manual, whether with a professional or alone, is to empower parents to help their child and, in so doing, help themselves. By helping their child and by conducting the 12-minute therapy sessions daily (for at least 5 of 7 days per week), not only does the child start producing word approximations and words but also, parents acquire the skills and confidence to manage their child during daily interactions. This component is essential and effectively accomplishes generalization of the newly acquired skills to routine daily parent-child interactions. Usually, 6 to 12 months are required to produce spontaneous appropriately constructed three-word sentences, although some children have taken longer and some as little as 3 months.

This program consists of two principal components: psychological development (of expressive language, cognition, object use, emotional regulation, and social behavior) and Learning Theory (Applied Behavior Analysis [ABA] to gain sufficient compliance from the child to permit new learning to occur). The principal assumption concerning the application of these procedures to children with autism is that development is arrested in children with autism, in large part, because the child avoids task demands. Simply put, most children with autism try to escape from things that they are asked to do. Our choice of the learning procedure for the application of ABA to produce compliance in the child is the Skinnerian procedure of shaping. This manual relies on the use of contingent positive reinforcement (rewards) to change behavior just as virtually all ABA approaches do. The application of rewards—generally praise, touch, and edibles—immediately following any response will increase the probability of that response whether you want it to or not. In that sense, contingent positive reinforcement is a law of behavior, just as gravity is a law of physics, and you violate it at your own peril. Laws of nature do not discriminate, they just are. Just as you would not drop a baby because it would fall, you should not reward undesirable behaviors such as tantrums because they will increase. Thus, be mindful about the application of rewards because they will increase behaviors that they follow whether you want them to or not. This manual helps parents to understand the application of learning principles to facilitate their child's development.

The systematic application of rewards to successive approximations of a desired goal is what distinguishes shaping from discrete trial training (DTT)—the repetition of trials until a set criterion (e.g., 80% correct) is reached. DTT is the most widely applied learning procedure in the treatment of autism. We believe that shaping has distinct advantages over DTT. First, shaping is faster, generally, and time is crucial if children with delayed development are to catch-up to their peers—the primary goal of early intervention. Second, DTT risks further stifling a child's intrinsic interest in a task that may occur initially with extrinsic rewards. Most children with autism have lost their intrinsic motivation, a capacity related to the pursuit of moderately discrepant information and that is present at birth (cf., Kagan, 2002; Weiss, Zelazo & Swain, 1988). Instead, they often wander aimlessly rather than display sustained attention and interest to a task. It is a challenge for a treatment program to re-ignite intrinsic motivation in a child who has autism, rather than to discourage it.

The three factors mentioned here, parent-implemented therapy, a broad emphasis on development as the content of treatment, and a reliance on the Skinnerian learning procedure of shaping to produce behavioral change, are the things that distinguish this approach to teach children with autism to speak from other manuals. The result has been typically developing expressive language in the majority of children with autism with whom the manual has been used under supervision. This is why we have agreed to re-issue this manual. Finally, we acknowledge that the ultimate criterion for acceptance of a finding is the publication of results in peer-reviewed journals, not only in our own authored book. We have substantial data sets that are in preparation and that will be submitted for publication over the next two-to three years. These findings not only include the development of expressive language but the role of development in multiple domains and learning principles (mostly shaping and the application of schedules of reinforcement) for use in the treatment of children with autism. In the interim, the re-issuance of this manual may help some of the increasing number of families confronted with the trauma of autism and the limited or ineffective resources available to them.

—PRZ, August 18, 2005

REFERENCES

Kagan, J. (2002). Surprise, Uncertainty, and Mental Structures. Cambridge, MA: Harvard University Press.

Weiss, M. J., Zelazo, P. R., & Swain, I. U. (1988). Newborn response to auditory stimulus discrepancy. Child Development, 59, 530–541.

Acknowledgments

A project of this magnitude, and we believe quality, could not have been completed without the cooperation and support of many individuals. Certainly, parents have been the cornerstone of this particular manual from its very inception on through its validation. We owe a particular debt of gratitude to a small nucleus of extraordinarily dedicated and cooperative parents of children with delays of unknown etiology who worked with us prior to the commencement of the validation project. We are particularly indebted to Mrs. K. P. whose extraordinary patience, diligence, and kind feedback helped to determine the salient features needed to advance her daughter to the next highest level of language development. The experience and knowledge gained from these highly motivated parents formed the foundation from which the present project was cast. Their dedication to their children, tolerance with our early inexperience, and commitment to do what they could to help their children, was heroic. We hope they gain satisfaction in the knowledge that their efforts helped the parents and children who participated in the validation project, and may help to spare other parents and children anguish in the future.

Of course, we want to thank the conscientious parents who participated for the 2½ years required of each family for testing the validity of these procedures. As the results of that investigation reveal, often parents are a child's best therapist. Successes in the validation project indicate that parents are prepared to accept responsibility for their child's developmental outcome and are willing and able to implement behavioral changes to meet that end. Their performance should encourage professionals to view parents of handicapped children as active and competent participants in their child's behavioral therapy.

There are numerous individuals who helped to test and refine these procedures. We want to thank Maryann Collins, Susan Coley, and Marguerite Randolph who served successive terms as head research assistant, a euphemism for assistant project director, during the 6½ years that it took to reach this point. They bore major responsibility during the validation project, but also took a personal interest in this manual to reverse noncompliant behaviors and facilitate productive language. Kathleen O'Leary, Noreen Carey-Neville, and Jean Soo Hoo, assisted some of our parents as home visitors and provided detailed helpful feedback on the treatment procedures themselves. Helene Chaika, Tom Chiodo, Kathleen Kurowski, Michael Weiss, and Maureen Whalen helped during various phases with the documentation and refinement of these procedures, and Michael Weiss prepared the subject index. Mary Anne Glennon assisted with the difficult task of coordinating schedules for subject testings and typed earlier drafts of this manual. Lucy Kuder competently typed the "final version" of this manuscript several times.

Nancy Kearsley and Paula Menyuk provided critical feedback on earlier drafts of this manuscript and helped to steer us away from some of the pitfalls inherent in our unavoidable travels into the disciplines of speech pathology and psycholinguistics, respectively. We thank them for their competent and valuable guidance.

The research establishing the validity of the procedures described in this manual and the refinement of these treatment procedures was supported directly by grants from the Office of Special Education (#G00760379), and the Carnegie Corporation of New York and, in part, by grants from the Division of Family Health Services, Massachusetts Department of Public Health, and the March of Dimes, National Foundation for Birth Defects. The authors acknowledge that the statements and views expressed are solely their responsibility. However, our obligation to our funding sources go beyond a mere formal acknowledgment. From its very inception, the research establishing the validity of both the diagnostic and treatment procedures benefited immeasurably from the intelligent advice and unwavering support of our project officer at the Office of Special Education, Dr. James Hamilton, and the Section Head, Dr. Max Mueller. Their perceptions of research priorities and mechanisms for implementing and monitoring this research not only were consonant with our own, but their interactions with us were intellectually stimulating, enjoyable, and satisfying. We want to thank them and Dr. Kenneth McLaughlin, who replaced Dr. Hamilton as Project Director during the final days of our funding period, for their support, wisdom, and friendship. We also owe a particularly large debt to Mrs. Barbara Finberg, Vice President of the Carnegie Corporation of New York, who will forever remain a heroine in our eyes. Her timely stewardship and unwavering support over the past 1½ years literally made the completion of this manual possible.

We thank all these individuals deeply. This project has been our preoccupation for the past 6½ years, yet many tasks remain before we finish. Nonetheless, at this phase, P.Z. and R.K. want to thank their wives and children and J.U. thanks her husband for their tolerance of our obsession to translate basic psychological research into applicable procedures. We hope that the completion of this phase, marking a station along the way, will make the remainder of our journey lighter.

LEARNING TO SPEAK:
A Manual For Parents

1 Overview

It is not surprising that the child's first steps and first words are celebrated events in the minds of parents and treated as major developmental landmarks by professionals. The ability to walk upright and to use speech to communicate distinguishes humans from other species. The potential for acquiring these skills is part of the biological heritage that accompanies the child's entry into the world. The age at which the underlying capacity for these skills emerges is relatively constant for children in most societies. However, the age at which this capacity is expressed with sufficient skill to allow the child to explore the environment and communicate with parents and others varies greatly. An increasing number of researchers are acknowledging that the underlying competence appears to be dictated, in part, by a maturing mental ability. The expression of the underlying central processing ability appears to be influenced to a greater extent by environmental opportunities than the maturation of the mental ability itself. This need for a supportive environment to complement a biological readiness appears to be true for speech. Whereas 1-year-old children may be "biologically ready" to produce single words, not all children announce their first birthday by demonstrating this uniquely human characteristic. For most, the delay, if any, is minimal. Single words appear, are soon joined by others words, and speech emerges as the child's primary vehicle for communicating thoughts, feelings, and a growing understanding of the environment. But for others, the delay may be prolonged. When the normal course of speech development is disrupted

1

or delayed, the delay becomes a source of growing concern in the minds of parents. To compound matters, delayed speech is often viewed as evidence of potential intellectual impairment by the professional community.

Facility with talking, the ability to comprehend and carry out verbal instructions, and/or the size of a child's spoken vocabulary are not necessarily valid measures of the young child's intellect. However, the fact remains that in our society and in much of the Western world, by the time children reach the age of 3, and increasingly thereafter, they are judged by their capacity to use language to express their thoughts and needs. The truth of this generally held impression is confirmed by the assumptions underlying the majority of standard tests used to measure the intellectual and social abilities of young children. By age 3, tests of children's mental development become heavily laden with items that require the ability to speak, to understand language, and to comply with verbal instructions. Moreover, the ability to talk appears to make the onset of reading more likely, less problematic, and easier. Not only is language of monumental significance in its own right, but in our society it is usually a natural prerequisite to the acquisition of reading and writing. Speech delays may diminish spontaneously as the child approaches school age, but nonetheless, they place the child at risk for delayed reading readiness. The problem may change its complexion, but it does not disappear, for tests given to older children rely on reading and writing facility. Thus, productive language often serves directly or indirectly as a measure of the child's underlying intellectual abilities. Despite logical limitations, problems with productive language continue to forecast problems in the elementary school years.

Productive language, roughly equivalent to a child's speech, can be distinguished from what a child knows or comprehends about language. Just because a child does not say something does not mean that he or she does not know that word, grammatical structure, or function. Moreover, comprehension often appears to develop more rapidly than production. Frequently children who are learning to talk seem to know more than they can say. Nonetheless, what a child says is one way to learn what a child knows about language. There is a limit to what we can learn about a child's language knowledge from simply observing his or her behavior when there is no speech. Clearly productive language is important on many levels.

The importance of productive language for normal development cannot be overemphasized. The judgment that speech-delayed children are at risk for general developmental delays has some validity. A child who is not talking is at a real disadvantage relative to normally speaking peers,

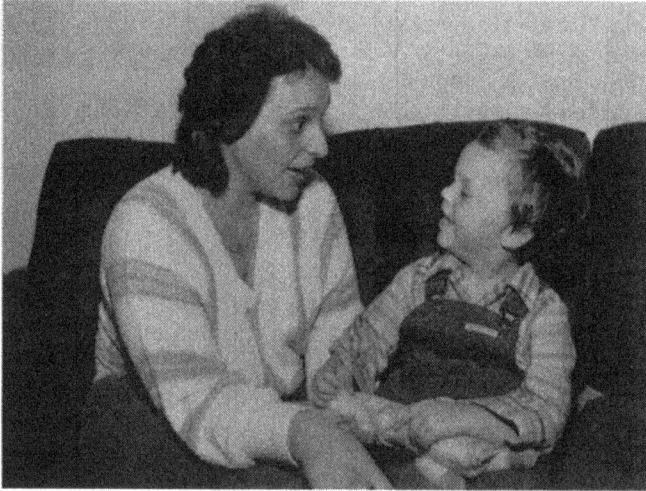

not only in preschool, but at home. It is no great revelation that the ability to talk can make interaction with adults and children easier and more productive. Asking questions, clarifying thoughts, and articulating one's own understanding can produce intellectual growth even at the preschool and toddler levels. This growth is a direct result of the ability to express oneself verbally.

In addition, there are social consequences to productive language delays. The speech-delayed child is often ignored by peers and, if accepted momentarily, often does not appreciate the rules of peer interaction. Frequently, either rejection or aggression is produced. If the developmental delays that often accompany speech delays continue, subsequent social experiences will bring even greater problems. Isolation, embarrassment, shyness, and lack of confidence can occur on one extreme, and unruly, unmanageable, hyperactive behavior on the other. Paradoxically, some developmentally delayed children express both these extremes.

An accomplishment of such importance as the acquisition of productive language deserves special attention, and those factors that influence this critical aspect of early development should not be left to chance alone. Both parents and professionals go to great lengths to protect and promote children's physical growth and development. They use their knowledge of nutrition, immunization, and physical exercise to insure that the underlying capacity for normal physical and motor development will be realized. Parents encourage their children to reach, grasp, crawl, walk, run, skip, climb, and explore the world. Parents and professionals also pay close attention to children's diets to insure that they receive proper nutrition. It is equally appropriate to use our knowledge of language, cognitive, and behavioral development to stimulate the development of talking directly and, through greater facility with productive language, to promote children's intellectual development indirectly.

There are facts about the development of productive language that can be used to facilitate talking among speech-delayed children. Some conditions carry a higher probability for eliciting speech from a child than do others. For example, there are times during the child's acquisition of productive language when one form of speech is more likely to occur spontaneously than another. There are particular reactions to a child's early efforts to produce sounds that render the development of words more likely. There is knowledge about the natural course of language learning that makes it possible to identify a child's current level of language development, anticipate the next level, and facilitate its achievement.

The material presented in this manual sets forth a simple program that we have developed, based on research, that combines both the naturally occurring biological and behavioral factors that contribute to the onset and facilitate the development of talking. The program described in this manual approaches this naturally occurring process from the child's view and sets conditions that are more likely to make speech, rather than nonverbal behaviors, the dominant mode of communication. Once a certain level of speech complexity has been achieved by the child, the ability to communicate is in itself such a satisfying experience for the child that the acquisition of increasingly sophisticated language is virtually assured. It is during the early stages of learning to speak that special emphasis may be needed either to insure that this critical facet of development gets off to a good start or to overcome delays and redirect the child back to a verbal means of language development.

The suggestion that both biological and behavioral factors may influence language acquisition can be illustrated by the acquisition of the child's first words. There is evidence that toward the end of the first year of life the infant undergoes a major maturational change in intellectual ability that makes many new developments possible. This change is illustrated clearly in the quality of children's play. An 8-month-old infant uses toys in a stereotyped manner—mouthing, waving, and banging them indiscriminately. However, a 12-month-old infant knows the uses for these same objects and may put a telephone to his or her ear and babble, or roll a car on its wheels. It appears that the same change in mental ability that makes functional play possible sets the stage for the child's first words. It is not appropriate to encourage first words before there is evidence of this change in mental ability.

Thus, most children begin to produce their first spoken words within a month or so of their first birthday. Similarly, it is probably not by accident that *mama* and *dada* are often among the first words spoken. They are easy sounds that children produce spontaneously and that parents model, repeat, and reward with smiles, hugs, and unrestrained enthusiasm. The effect of this immediate positive response (reward) by the parent for a sound (word approximation) that the child produced (a contingent reaction) increases the chance that the child will say the word again. This naturally occurring sequence of events illustrates how the environment interacts with the child's biological readiness to encourage words and facilitate the further acquisition of spoken language.

In addition to the maturational change at 1 year that influences a child's readiness for the onset of his or her first words, there are other broad developmental influences. Later, there is a clear development from simple to complex spoken language, which is described in this chapter, that guides the progression of targeted language throughout this program. There is a recognition that parents have much more influence as attached persons in the child's life than do strangers and, as such, have greater leverage as teachers during the second and third years of life. Similarly, there is an appreciation for the fact that a speech-delayed child who has begun to talk will require some time and exposure before talking comfortably to strangers, or to preschool teachers. Generalization of the child's newly acquired language from the "teaching sessions" to daily activities in the home and from the home to less familiar situations will play a central role in this program. Broadly speaking, generalization and children's shyness in strange situations are developmental phenomena that influence productive language acquisition, particularly for speech-delayed children.

However, one of the most important biological or maturational considerations that guides this program is the recognition that the child is an active contributor to the language acquisition process. Children develop rules about language acquisition and use those rules creatively. For example, a child may say "foots" rather than "feet," even though he or she may not have heard "foots" used before. Instead, the child generalized a rule about regular plural formation to an irregular case where it does not apply.

The primary implication of this biological contribution for this program is that children are treated as active participants who do not have to be taught each step along the way. For example, if children have the underlying competence to support speech, no separate time is spent teaching language comprehension or understanding. Comprehension is expected to come in the time needed to learn to say the word. Similarly, if word approximations are possible and the child has a small spoken vocabulary, words rather than babbling are encouraged. Initially, meaningful word approximations even with poor articulation, are encouraged. Thus, if a child with a six-word vocabulary reliably says *ar* for *car,* it is acceptable

TABLE 1.1

Age Months	Years	Nonlinguistic Development	Linguistic Development	Vocabulary
1		Reflexive crying and noncry comfort sounds		
2		Private and social babbling		
5-6		Vocal play		
10		Echolalia (imitating self and others)		
12			First words - holophrastic speech	10-20 words
	1½	Jargon (practicing fluency)		50-250 words
	2		Telegraphic speech - joining 2 words	All vowels
	2½		3-word utterances, inflection appears	450 words
	3		Complete simple sentences with pronouns	
	3½		Compound sentences - 3-4 word utterances	800 words
	4		Mastery of inflections - 5-word utterances	p, b, m, h, w, n, ng
	4½			k, j, g, f, d
	5		Articulation 90% intelligible	
	5½			t, r, sh, v, l, s
	6		Compound-complex sentences	
	8½			Occasional misarticulation of: tw, dw, bl, kl, fl, gl, pl, sl, br, kr, dr, fr, gr, pr, tr, thr, sk, sm, sn, st, kw

Adapted from: Wilkinson, L. C., & Saywitz, K. Theoretical bases of language and communication development in preschool children. In M. Lewis and L. T. Taft (Eds.), *Developmental Disabilities: Theory, Assessment, and Intervention*, New York: S.P. Medical & Scientific Books, 1982.

during the initial stages. In our view, the gains resulting from the use of an intelligible word approximation for a meaningful object far exceed the disadvantages of a misarticulation at this point in development. Improved articulation is encouraged later.

Knowledge of the principles of behavior that are used with this program increase the probability that a child will use verbal rather than nonverbal means to communicate. There is a vast amount of literature in psychology demonstrating that the use of rewards can increase the likelihood that one behavior rather than another will occur. The procedures described in this manual rely on the biological foundations that establish the patterns and limits for normal language acquisition as well as the use of rewards. Contingent rewards provide the incentive that is essential for promoting the normal sequences for productive language among speech-delayed children. The rewards act to change the child's reliance on one habit, such as crying, which may prove counterproductive to speech acquisition, to another response, such as saying *drink,* which may promote a normal pattern of development.

In the case of a child whose overall development is proceeding normally, knowledge of the biological and behavioral bases for the acquisition of productive language can remove the element of chance from the process and make success more likely with greater ease. Thus, knowledge of the normal sequence of language development, shown in Table 1.1, can allow parents of normal children to take advantage of the child's natural readiness for talking by encouraging the appropriate kinds of production at various levels of development. Moreover, this knowledge can increase the likelihood that parents will provide a language environment that will establish an early and rich foundation for subsequent langauge development.

The language sequence and milestones listed in Table 1.1 are only approximations; there is substantial variability in language development among children. Exceptions will occur. Some children may develop several two or even three word utterances well before two years of age, for example. Some children may have only five words, whereas others may have 50 words by 18 months. However, in general, the sequence outlined in Table 1.1 provides a reasonable approximation of the ages and order of language acquisition.

FOR WHOM IS THE MANUAL INTENDED?

This manual is intended to provide parents with an effective, efficient method for increasing the young child's disposition to use words and sentences to communicate. It is designed for use with intellectually normal children whose speech delays are not a valid indication of mental retardation. In our own research, this determination was made by establishing age-appropriate information-processing ability for specifically designed visual and auditory events despite delays on traditional tests of infant-toddler development. We have shown that this program works most effectively with children whose delayed langauge may depress their scores on conventional tests and mask their normal intellectual potential.

This manual is not appropriate for children with physical disorders such as a serious, uncorrectable hearing loss that may be accompanied by impaired language learning. Normal or corrected hearing is a necessary prerequisite for this productive language program. Many of the children that we studied experienced recurrent ear infections that resulted in temporary periods of impaired hearing. Our procedures were highly effective with these children when their infections were resolved.

This manual is not suited for children whose mental age, as determined by a qualified clinical psychologist, is less than 12 months. Also, it is advisable that parents of children whose delays in mental age exceed 10 months should seek the assistance and supervision of a qualified speech pathologist, psychologist, or early educator for their use of the procedures described in this manual. Children with delays in excess of 10 months may present too great a challenge to their parents, who may need the advice and assistance of a professional to guide them with this manual.

Intellectually Normal Children with Speech Delays

Parents often describe the speech-delayed child as one who understands much of what is said but fails to speak. Such children can frequently communicate by using nonverbal behaviors such as gesturing without words, grabbing, crying, and having tantrums to indicate their needs, wants, likes, and dislikes. Pointing and gesturing are normal occurrences during early langauge learning, but the child who relies totally on nonverbal behaviors soon becomes limited in his or her communications. The exclusive reliance on nonverbal behaviors may, in fact, impede the learning of productive language. Such children have a limited number of words at their command. It is not unusual for an 18-month-old child to have no spoken words and the 32-month-old to have a limited usable vocabulary of a dozen poorly articulated words. In addition to the limited vocabulary, the children for whom this manual is intended frequently resist their parents' attempts to elicit speech. This resistance, either actively expressed, as in tantrums, or passively conveyed, as in quietly turning away, often makes important contributions to the child's overall delay in learning to speak.

We believe, on the basis of our research and clinical experience, that delays in learning to speak may place the child at considerable risk for further developmental complications. This concern is shared by speech pathologists who caution that the 30-month-old who has not acquired a normal level of productive language may subsequently have difficulties in such language-related skills as reading.

At least three factors contribute to this shared concern. First, the standard developmental tests used to estimate the young child's intellectual competence rely heavily on the words that a child understands and uses. Thus, failure to pass language items on developmental tests may cast doubt on a child's intellectual ability. Second, the longer children persist (and are successful) in using nonverbal means to communicate, the more difficult it becomes to "unlearn" nonverbal behaviors and to redirect the child back to a verbal mode of language expression. Third, speech-delayed children do not always spontaneously overcome their language deficit. Rather, the weight of evidence indicates that with increasing age, failure to acquire normal patterns of speech and language results in a further separation between speech-delayed children and their normal peers. This tendency to fall further behind may extend into other areas and skills essential for successful school performance, such as reading and writing, even after talking begins.

Children from Disrupted Environments

There are several categories of children who may not be exposed to normal opportunities for language stimulation. Research has shown that, on the average, some environments may increase the likelihood that difficulties with language development will occur. Children in these environments are at risk for productive language delays and articulation problems because of inopportune or unfavorable circumstances. There are many ways that the chances for delays with speech and language development can increase, including multiple births, extremely large families, prolonged hospitalizations, recurrent ear infections during the period when talking emerges, and a host of other medical difficulties. These environmental factors may result in parents unintentionally altering the demands that they normally place on their children. Circumstances that expose parents to periodic or continuing stress may seriously disrupt the home environment. For example, marital discord, loss of income, or a death in the family, can temporarily strain parental ability to cope with the demands of daily living and may impair a child's opportunity to learn to speak. However, in each instance, only the probability or chance for difficulty with language acquisition is increased; a speech delay is not an automatic outcome. Two children from apparently similar environments with identical presenting problems may turn out differently: One may develop delays, whereas the other may not. Research is beginning to show that the environment that aids or impedes language acquisition is highly specific. Increasingly, it appears that not only must there be a cognitive readiness, but that contingent responsiveness by the child's caregivers may also influence the onset of talking.

Psychologists are beginning to discover that environments for individual children within the same family can be markedly different. A recent study of adopted children illustrates the kinds of differences between children within the same family that may lead to sharp differences in language development. Of the numerous environmental factors that could possibly influence language development by 1 year of age, only two proved to be important in a study of 50 adopted children. The mother's imitation of infant vocalization and her contingent responsiveness to her child's vocalizations and verbalizations were the only environmental variables that correlated with the rate of the child's communicative development. These two maternal behaviors are similar and illustrate the benefit of responding positively (with reward) and contingently (immediately) to the child's efforts at speech. They also illustrate one way that parent-child interactions within the same family can differ. It is possible to develop a pattern of responding to verbalizations by one child and a different pattern of responding to gesturing and crying by another. These different patterns can unintentionally encourage two different communication styles. It is important to emphasize that parents are not at fault here; rather, they are victims of circumstances that were previously undiscovered. On the positive side, there is something that can be done to reverse the difficulty.

Multiple Births and Large Families.   The demands for feeding, bathing, diapering, and day-to-day supervision are increased with multiple births such as twins. For example, physical caregiving responsibilities are doubled with twins, but there is only a limited amount of time and energy available to parents each day. Thus, the total amount of time available for playing games, stimulating verbal interaction, and encouraging the child's achievements is further divided by a factor of 2 because parent-child interaction is a one-to-one experience. Relative to a single-born infant, each twin may have only ¼ the time available for one-to-one parent-child interaction. The situation is more difficult for parents of triplets or quadruplets. Of course, parents manage to compensate; somehow they find the time to encourage normal psychological development. The main point is that the demands on parents of twins are much greater. Procedures to help them carry out their responsibilities more efficiently are usually welcomed.

Time becomes a precious commodity for parents of large families as well as for those with multiple births, and there is a tremendous need to be effective and efficient in meeting both the physical and psychological needs of the children growing up within such a family environment. Language delays are more likely among children of multiple births than singletons and are not infrequent among the younger children in large families. In some cases, the delays associated with multiple births may be related to other problems, such as prematurity, which often accompanies multiple births. However, the majority of delays in productive language found in such children often appear to be related to experience rather than to any underlying medical or neurological deficit.

Similar to multiple births, children in large families who share parental time and energy with older siblings may not have access to the amount of attention available to the first- and second-born children. In addition, older siblings frequently talk for the "baby" and by so doing decrease the need for the younger child to learn to use words and acquire the basic language skills that emerge during the early years. It is important to emphasize that it is not simply the size of the family that places an individual child at risk for delays in speech. Most children from large families show normal development. Rather, it is the specific circumstances that surround a particular child during the time of early language learning that may interfere with the acquisition of speech. The procedures described in this manual allow parents to create a language learning environment that makes the most of opportunities to encourage speech systematically, consistently, and efficiently.

Prolonged Interruption of Normal Environments.   Children afflicted with long-term physical disorders or those requiring repeated hospitalization frequently encounter significant disruptions in their contact with parents. An 18-month-old child who develops dehydration from a prolonged gastrointestinal illness, possibly with complications, may require a disruptive and threatening hospitalization. Even a 2-week stay may induce a temporary developmental setback, including a regression in language development. The child's vulnerability to unfamiliar situations at this age can result in a frightening experience that may lead to withdrawal. Moreover, despite attempts of nurses and other hospital staff to lessen the impact of such unavoidable separations, the unfamiliar hospital staff is at a disadvantage with the child who has a fear of strangers. In addition, the hospital staff does not always provide contingent responsiveness for the child's verbalizations. The medical or surgical problem that caused the hospitalization may impose major caregiving demands on both parents and professionals. In these instances, there is often little time for attention to such "non–life-threatening matters" as learning to speak.

It is difficult for parents to impose the same level of demand for age-appropriate performance on a child with a major physical disorder as they would with a physically normal child. The development of productive language appears to be particularly vulnerable to this tendency to lower demands and expectations in the face of serious and continuing medical problems. Divorce or unexpected loss of a parent or sibling may result in a more prolonged interruption of what may have been a normal and nurturant environment. Once again, the need is for an efficient method for stimulating and sustaining the early phases of language development. Contingent positive responsiveness to the child's speech appears to be one efficient procedure.

Intellectually Normal Children in a Normal Environment

Language is a central aspect of the child's early development. Its acquisition should neither be taken for granted nor left to chance alone. Knowledge of the natural course of productive language acquisition can help parents include in their daily interactions with their child those behaviors that complement the underlying biological readiness for language development. For example, if a child's vocabulary is limited to six words, it would not be appropriate to attempt two- or three-word phrases. One reason is that the acquisition of productive language follows a predictable pattern as shown in Table 1.1, even though there is considerable variation in the ages at which children reach different levels of acquisition. Nevertheless, these levels become manifest in an orderly sequence with early abilities setting the stage for more sophisticated levels of language development. Thus, parents of a child with a limited vocabulary of single-word utterances should stimulate their child's talking by expanding the vocabulary of single words rather than encouraging two- and three-word sentences. Encouraging two-word sentences is more effective when the child is reliably producing about 60 single-word statements. At this point, two-word phrases become an appropriate target because they coincide with the next phase of language learning.

One of the goals of this manual is to present a task in language acquisition that is appropriate for each child's particular level of language learning from single words to multiple-word productions. Knowledge of early language development and an understanding of various behavioral principles can make it easier for parents to foster the acquisition of productive language efficiently and naturally. Knowing what to expect and how to go about achieving that expectation is a basic part of raising children in general and an important component of the child's language development in particular.

Our society emphasizes children's facility with productive language in both formal and informal settings. Children are judged informally by peers, neighbors, and teachers (even at the preschool level) on their capacity to speak and their facility with the use of words. Speech and language are used to evaluate children formally on standardized tests of intelligence. Because of this widespread emphasis on language development, parents of normal children may wish to take advantage of the knowledge and procedures contained in this manual that may contribute to a good start in the development of productive language.

However, we urge one caution: Parents of normal children should not push too hard or make unrealistic demands in an attempt to produce a "genius." For example, it would be inappropriate to attempt to elicit speech from a 6-month-old infant, because children normally are not ready to talk until about 12 months. The entire process set forth in this manual emphasizes a delicate match between children's current language readiness and the target material that the parent should attempt to elicit and reward, either within a formal productive language training session or as part of their normal daily interactions with the child. Thus, we urge readers not to make excessive and unrealistic demands. On the contrary, a primary value of this manual for parents of normal children is that it can provide a guide for determining more accurately which demands are realistic at different phases of the child's acquisition of speech. It is important to keep in mind that there is much variability in language development among children. Parents of normally developing children need not become overly anxious about talking; rather, knowledge and understanding of the natural course of productive language development should reduce much of this common concern.

At present, we advise that the procedures described in this manual be used primarily with intellectually normal speech-delayed children and children at risk for language delays. It is possible that parents of intellectually normal children with normal language developing within a nonrisk environment may find this manual useful as a guide for understanding, tracking, and optimizing their child's development. Whether parents of normal children elect to use the more formal language teaching procedures that are recommended for speech-delayed children or to modify the procedures for use in a more naturalistic situation is a choice that we leave to the parents themselves. The manner in which parents of normal children choose to apply the information and procedures contained in this manual is less important than the recognition that they can favorably influence their child's talking through an increased awareness of language development.

We have used the procedures described in this manual with a limited number of children afflicted with significant developmental handicaps including mental impairment as well as major physical disabilities. However, the application of this language-stimulation program to physically and mentally impaired children requires further research in order to determine its efficacy and limitations. We do not recommend it for these children at present.

MATURATIONAL AND ENVIRONMENTAL FOUNDATIONS

Unlike many theoretical and research statements about the acquisition of productive language, we acknowledge both maturational and behavioral determinants of speech. Either view alone appears to be inadequate to produce the changes that we sought. It is our experience that a child's speech will not automatically unfold if naturally occurring rewards, particularly adult responsiveness to speech, do not occur. Contingent social rewards are a key ingredient that defines a "normal environment" irrespective of social class, education, income, number of children in the family, and a host of other possible variables. It is our experience that if productive language is to be acquired, certain social and naturally occurring nonsocial consequences to a child's early attempts to talk must occur.

As we have mentioned, the children for whom this manual was initially prepared were cognitively intact, and thus, they possessed the intellectual skills necessary to sustain speech. Typically, they were not identified as language delayed until at least 20 months of age and often not until they had approached their third birthday. These children came from families varying in social class, education, income, and family size, and they were not neglected by their parents. The majority of parents expressed concern about their child's lack of productive language. Moreover, many of the children who were subsequently diagnosed as language delayed had, in the past, acquired a handful of words that for a variety of reasons were subsequently lost. One disturbing question can be raised: What prevented the normal course of productive language acquisition among these children?

A partial answer to this question can be found in the belief held widely by parents and professionals involved with the care of children: When children are ready to talk, they will do so. Thus, the concerns of parents of a 2-year-old who is not talking are often disregarded or attributed to overly anxious parents. The normal variability in language learning is used to allay parent's fears, and the often quoted phrase "Albert Einstein didn't talk until he was 4" is brought forth as further evidence of the parent's unrealistic concern. Unfortunately, the passage of time alone may not result in the acquisition of productive language, but rather may create greater difficulty for the child who must eventually unlearn nonverbal means of communication. Judging from our experience, the number of children who suddenly, at age 4, begin speaking in complex grammatically correct sentences are probably as unusual as Einstein himself. It is more likely that talking will emerge eventually but will be delayed and/or disordered for a period. Moreover, when productive language develops late, the onset of subsequent related skills such as reading, are also delayed.

The success of the approach outlined in this manual provides another clue as to why some children may develop language delays. It appears that the sample of speech-delayed children studied in our research experienced a subtle, yet powerful, breakdown in the naturally occurring environmental consequences to their use of speech. This "breakdown" is neither intentional nor done out of a lack of concern. On the contrary, it appears that there is often a great concern for the child's development that provokes the parent to anticipate the child's every wish and to avoid all but minimal demands for age-appropriate behavior in general and speech in particular. In retrospect, it is easy to see how this may happen. For example, a child who has been hospitalized early on for gastroenteritis and resultant dehydration may become a great concern for the parents. During the illness, the child may have cried excessively because of discomfort and pain. It is appropriate for parents to hold and comfort the child under these circumstances, but if continued beyond the period of illness, a habit to communicate through crying may take hold. Even if the child had already acquired a limited number of words and was just beginning to speak, this shift in naturally occurring and well-intentioned behavioral contingencies could unintentionally encourage crying rather than talking as the primary means of communication.

There are numerous scenarios that could account for a breakdown in the naturally occurring parenting interactions that contain within them the rewards for speech. However, not all instances of productive language delay are due to environmental causes. Some language delays stem from an organic basis, such as an auditory processing problem, that may interfere with a child's ability to produce different linguistic categories and relations. In these cases, it is difficult for parents to anticipate the problems. Nevertheless, the contingent procedures in this manual may be useful to show these children how to parcel out and respond to linguistic information themselves.

The main point is that the change in parenting practices is subtle, highly specific, and draws attention to the enormous significance of contingent responsiveness to selectively reward and support the child's initial attempts at speech. The importance of contingent responsiveness for initial language acquisition was emphasized in the adoption study described earlier. The role of contingent reinforcement in the acquisition of speech and language has been argued with fervor by Professor B. F. Skinner of Harvard University. This manual demonstrates that, at least for the initial orientation toward verbal or nonverbal efforts, there is some validity for this view. However, this should not imply that talking develops through reward alone. There is no doubt that the child is an active contributor to the process of language acquisition in terms of both cognitive and linguistic underpinnings that enable the child to generate gramatical rules and create unique expressions such as "foots".

This manual also relies heavily on research into the biological foundations for language. Professors Lenneberg and Chomsky are two theorists, among others, who have argued strongly that language development has biological underpinnings. The program described in this manual acknowledges the importance of the child's own capacity to generate language. As indicated earlier, there appears to be a biologically influenced readiness for the development of talking that creates a capacity to understand that specific sounds are related to particular objects in the world.

There are changes in cognitive ability that occur toward the end of the first year of life that set the stage for language development. It appears as though children must have the capacity to generate specific associations rapidly in order to match sounds with their referents and produce those sounds appropriately. This cognitive change resembles the ability to generate ideas and is associated with the emergence of functional play in which objects begin to be used appropriately. A 9-month-old child will mouth, wave, and bang all objects indiscriminantly, whereas a 12-month-old will use them according to their adult defined purposes. For example, the older child will put a telephone receiver to his or her ear rather than to his or her mouth and will babble appropriately. This knowledge of functions is similar to the intellectual ability needed for the onset of first words. Until there is evidence of this underlying cognitive ability, either through functional play, a developmental examination, a test of information processing ability, or the child's own display of several words, procedures to encourage talking may not be appropriate.

The increasing speed with which single words are acquired also appears to be a contribution of the child's underlying cognitive capacity. The pattern of increasing complexity from single words to multiple-word sentences, although not followed strictly, appears with sufficient regularity and universality to imply an underlying maturational contribution. Finally, the increasing abstractness of the words that the child is able to comprehend and produce implies that the child has not simply been reinforced by environmental consequences to utter appropriate sounds but, rather, is bringing an increasingly sophisticated cognitive competence to the task of acquiring language. Moreover, contingent rewards do not provide a convincing explanation of children's comprehension of language or their ability to acquire the underlying knowledge and rules that govern the use of words and phrases. Thus, it appears to be neither by biology nor by behavioral consequences alone that the child gains the capacity to produce language of increasing complexity.

The organization of the manual conforms to a developmental timetable for language readiness that is approximated in Table 1.1. Thus, it is necessary to establish that a particular child's intellectual ability is in excess of 12 months before these procedures are attempted. If this first criterion is met, the sessions begin with single-syllable concrete nouns, which name objects commonly found in the child's environment, that already exist in the child's vocabulary. These simple words serve as the "target" for the individual language teaching sessions. It is common for children's first words to be one-syllable nouns such as *ball, car, eye,* and *nose*. These often are followed by or occur with two-syllable nouns such as *baby, mama,* and *daddy*. Simple verbs such as *drink, walk,* and *sit* and functional words such as *out, up, please,* and *more* usually follow. Possessives often occur before more complex and abstract forms of speech, including concepts such as *under, beside,* and *over*. Adjectives, adverbs, and prepositions generally occur much later, often after two-word phrases are used. This progression is not a firm one followed by all children, and many children may show some departure from it, but in general, there is conformity. This pattern takes on greater significance in this program for facilitating productive language because it provides a guiding framework for selecting target words to teach during the training sessions.

Because one of the underlying principles of the program is to maximize the child's experience of success, words that are already in the child's vocabulary are used to begin and close each training session. New words that expand the child's existing vocabulary are introduced during the middle portions, and the repetition of already acquired words makes it possible to begin and end on a positive note. As the productive vocabulary approaches 50 or 60 different words, the target changes, and two-word productions become the focus of the teaching sessions. The combination of words from a child's existing vocabulary into meaningful phrases that conform to the syntax and grammar of the language being learned gradually dominates the 12-minute teaching sessions. The expansion of the existing vocabulary combined with a lengthening of the phrases into three- and four-word sentences characterizes the final stages of the productive language program.

The developmental progression of productive language acquisition has other characteristics that are useful for this program. For example, the combination of words into meaningful phrases appears to follow a relatively ordered progression. Generally, the simple naming of objects precedes questions about objects. Approximations of words often precede their correct pronunciation and frequently require repeated practice before they occur. Single words may be produced correctly when said alone, yet mispronounced when combined into two- and three-word phrases. The shift from single-word to two-word phrases represents a major developmental landmark. The extension into three-, four-, and five-word phrases emerges as a less distinct phase of language learning. Many linguists argue that there is no three-, four-, or five-word phase of language acquisition, but rather a rapid acquisition of increasingly complex utterances.

The developmental foundations for language have been used to organize the manual, but the procedures adopted to activate this underlying maturational readiness are based on the science of behavior. The success of contingent positive reward or operant conditioning has been demonstrated repeatedly in psychology under a variety of circumstances. Briefly, this principle states that if a pleasurable outcome follows a desired behavior, the probability that the desired behavior will recur is increased. Thus, if a small edible reward (a raisin) is given to a child after he or she utters an approximation of the word *more,* the probability that the child will say *more* again is increased. Throughout the productive language training sessions, this fact remains unchanged. A form of speech is identified as the targeted outcome for a particular child at a specific point in time. If the desired word or words are spoken, the child's speech is followed by a pleasurable event—such as the presentation of an edible, social praise, and/or the object or outcome requested when possible.

A HYPOTHETICAL EXAMPLE

In order for a child's talking to improve, the targeted outcome must become more complex as the language sessions progress. For example, if a 30-month-old boy, John, were to begin with a vocabulary of six words that were used rarely, the target or focus of emphasis for the rewards would be simply the repetition of this small vocabulary. The initial goal would be to increase John's disposition to use the words that are presently in his vocabulary. John may repeat these words a total of 85 times during the language teaching session when given praise, objects, and bits of chocolate for each production. It is easy to appreciate that unless the target or object of the reward changes, John's vocabulary will not increase. Therefore, the next step would be to add new one-syllable nouns during the middle of the session and to rehearse John's existing vocabulary at the beginning and end of the session. The use of familiar words to start and finish the sessions with the more difficult new words for the middle of the teaching episode insures that John will have a pleasurable experience.

Suppose that the six words in John's vocabulary were *ball, baby, dog, daddy, momma,* and *more* and that he could say the additional sounds "ca" and "oo." Following a week during which the six words in his vocabulary were repeated during the 12-minute sessions, it would be appropriate to target such words as *car, cup,* and *book* during the middle portions of the sessions. John's existing vocabulary would be used to begin and end the sessions with the more difficult new words introduced during the middle. In this way, John is likely to get off to a good start and to become pleased with himself at the end of the sessions after he has been "stretched" a bit during the middle. As John's vocabulary increased and as *car, cup,* and *book* were mastered, other new words could be added to the middle portion of the sessions. These now familiar words would then be moved to the beginning and the end of the sessions. As John's vocabulary increased to a total of about 60 words and as he acquired a variety of words representing verbs, adjectives, possessives, and simple concepts, the target would shift again so that two-word productions would become the focus during the middle portion of the sessions. When two-word productions occurred with ease, three-word sentences would become the target. All along, efforts would be made to insure that John's speech would generalize to other parts of the day and occur in natural contexts. Thus, the process of gradually increasing the complexity of the demands would continue until John spontaneously used three-, four-, and five-word sentences appropriately within a natural context. The day-to-day activities of this approach rely heavily on the use of contingent rewards for targeted speech, but it must be remembered that the nature of the target varies in accordance with the underlying developmental pattern for the acquisition of productive language.

Whereas a developmental model is used to organize this manual, a behavioral approach is used to stimulate children's access to the underlying heritage that is dependent on maturation. We recognize that these two positions are viewed by many as incompatible. However, it is helpful to focus on the practical need that this manual is intended to serve, namely, to channel the communicative efforts of children with speech delays into a verbal mode. The advantages derived from talking outweigh the continued use of a limited repertoire of gestures and nonverbal utterances. This combined behavioral-biological approach was derived from a purely pragmatic stance and, as such, lends partial credibility to the validity of both points of view. In our view, it is a tribute to the sciences of psychology, psycholinguistics, and linguistics that our pragmatic effort reveals little to contradict either theoretical position. Similarly, neither approach alone would have produced the continued gains that we have achieved by combining both points of view.

PARENTS AS THERAPISTS

Not only was it necessary to take both points of view seriously, but we had to realize, as others may have, that most children learn to speak from their parents—naturally and without special attention. The special attention for children with language delays does not negate the fact that parents are still the child's primary teachers. There are many reasons why parents are excellent therapists for their own children. The first and most important is that consistency in treatment is a central factor in the acquisition of productive language as it is in many other learning situations with children. Not only is consistency important for any one parent, but also between parents and other individuals such as a speech therapist. Second, parents have the primary responsibility for their own children and are highly motivated to help them. They are more interested in their own children than anybody else is, so they will work harder. Not only are parents attached to their children, but their children are attached to them. The practical consequence is that young children are more responsive to attached individuals than to strangers. A third reason why parents are ideal therapists is that they are with their children more than any other individual, particularly during the first 3 years of life. Because parents are strongly motivated, have a larger amount of time to devote, and have a far greater opportunity to provide consistent input over days, they are in an ideal position to help their children.

Consistency in treatment, even for brief periods of time each day as demonstrated by this speech acquisition program, is of paramount importance when complex habits are to be unlearned and new, equally complex behaviors acquired. By assisting parents to become therapists for their own children, counterproductive or inconsistent patterns of interaction that may have developed inadvertently can be corrected. Practice in responding contingently during the teaching sessions will help parents to generalize a contingent style of interaction to their daily activities. Thus, the effort of training parents to assist their own speech-delayed child yields an extraordinary benefit in improved parent-child interaction. Moreover, it has the potential of continuing to their mutual advantage long after the professional's involvement with the child or the daily teaching sessions have ceased.

In many instances, it is helpful or even desirable for parents to begin this program under the guidance of a speech therapist, psychologist, early educator, or other professional trained in the use of this approach. Here, the professional can train, advise, and explain the program to the parent and be available to solve problems, if they arise. Such an arrangement not only allows the professional to extend his or her influence in an effective way, but may also diminish the frustration that some professionals experience when there is only a finite amount of time and energy to devote to a seemingly infinite number of demanding problems.

Some parents prefer and others need the assistance of a professional guide to discuss and support their efforts at 2- or 3-week intervals during the initial phases of this program. In these cases, the efforts of both the professional and parent should converge harmoniously on setting conditions that will increase the probability that the child will begin to use speech. Other parents may choose to conduct the productive language program entirely on their own. In our experience, both situations have produced effective positive results. It appears to be up to the parents to determine whether they have the resources necessary to carry out the program on their own. In general, we have found that if a child's speech has been delayed until about 36 months of age, if the child's delay on conventional tests of intellectual development exceeds 10 months, or if moderate to severe behavioral problems develop as a consequence of the speech delay, it is best to conduct the program initially under the direction of a professional.

We learned during the treatment phase of our research that two conditions would have to be met if we were to use a child's best therapists—his or her parents. First, we discovered that most parents were not interested in theoretical discussions about language development—not even cursory theoretical discussions. Hence, it proved necessary to minimize our descriptions of the normal course of language development. Almost without exception, parents were interested in pragmatic considerations and the procedures that they could use to help their children. As a result, the procedures included in this program were forged by purely practical considerations. Those factors that facilitated language development from one level to the next in our pilot research were included in the program whether they were biological or behavioral in origin. Parents proved to us that even modest discussions of theory were unnecessary for the success of the program. Indeed, they taught us what many professionals already know: Parents need not have professional training in order to help their children to talk, even if those children are speech delayed.

Second, we learned that when parents were given an opportunity to participate in their child's treatment, not only were they impatient with theoretical discussions, but they wanted procedures that worked. Their primary concern was to help their children progress from a less to a more sophisticated level of language development. If parental cooperation was to be maintained, it was necessary to demonstrate progress over a brief period of time—about 2 to 3 weeks. Moreover, that progress had to continue. In effect, parental cooperation was contingent upon their child's progress. It was this criterion of progress that guided us in choosing factors essential to parental participation. The minimum number of variables that we can identify as necessary to encourage productive language development successfully are included in this manual. As a result, this manual raises important theoretical questions, but meets the pragmatic criterion of success. The procedures have been shown to work repeatedly.

SUPPORTING RESEARCH

We have seen a clinical sample of about 100 developmentally delayed children between 20 and 48 months of age. About 60% of this sample reversed their speech delays and achieved multiple-word sentences following varying degrees of intervention with these procedures. However, the clearest demonstration of the effectiveness of this productive language program occurred in a controlled experiment with 44 children who received parent-implemented treatment over a 10-month period.

The children were enrolled into our program at either 22 or 32 months of age and had clear delays with productive language that depressed their overall developmental scores. Formal evaluations revealed sizable delays on a widely used infant-toddler test of mental ability known as the Bayley Scales of Development. Delays in mental ability at 22 and 32 months averaged 8 and 11 months behind chronological age, respectively, implying that these children were mildly mentally retarded. Usually these children displayed immature play and were observed to be resistant to parental instruction in a controlled teaching situation.

Medical histories for these children revealed a variety of difficulties, but there was no evidence of congenital or acquired disorders that would produce mental retardation. There were no children with Down's syndrome or cerebral palsy, for example. A number of children were identified as "difficult" or colicky babies during the early months of life, and about ⅓ of the children in the sample experienced recurrent ear infections. Most of the children were slow to reach the usual developmental milestones, especially walking and talking. Many of the children had extensive medical evaluations that failed to produce a definitive reason for their delays, resulting in the classification of developmental delay of unknown etiology.

The principal objective of this experiment was to establish the validity or accuracy of newly created diagnostic procedures. We set out to discriminate children with intact intellectual ability from those with impaired intellectual ability in this sample using visual and auditory measures of information processing rather than traditional tests. In other words, we attempted to sort all the developmentally delayed children into one of two groups: intact versus impaired information processing. However, in order to prove that our diagnostic test correctly identified children with normal underlying competence despite the appearance of retardation, we needed to carry the experiment one step further. Because all of these children had real observable delays, an effective treatment procedure was needed. We reasoned that children with intact central processing ability would overcome their delays with effective treatment procedures because they had the underlying competence. Children with impaired central processing ability were not expected to improve measurably because they lacked the necessary underlying competence.

The productive language manual, with its attention to both resistant behavior and the facilitation of talking, served as the principal treatment procedure. Parents were given assistance and direction either through about seven office visits or through eight telephone calls and three evaluations during the 10-month treatment period. Results described here were based on standard developmental (Bayley Scale of Mental Development) and intelligence tests (Stanford–Binet, Form L-M, 1973 Revision) administered upon entry into the program, at the end of the treatment phase, and at 6- and 18-month follow-up evaluations. The predicted differential improvement between groups required both an accurate diagnosis and effective treatment procedures. Either factor alone was not likely to work.

The results for the 28-month period strongly supported the predictions. Children with intact processing ability reduced their delays from an average of 8 to .4 months. In contrast, children with impaired processing ability began at a lower level and increased their delays by 14 months from 15 to 29 months over the same period. Subsequent testing 24 months later indicated that, in general, differences between these two groups continued. It is an important finding for parents of children with developmental delays of unknown etiology that about three of every four children in our sample (77%) displayed intact central processing ability. It is equally important that 61% of these intact children eliminated their delays on conventional tests 28 months after entering the program. They achieved mental age scores that were equal to or greater than their chronological ages using this productive language manual.

These results are all the more striking when one realizes that in order for delays to be reduced, a developmentally delayed child must develop at a pace faster than normal for a period of time. The success of this experiment strongly illustrates the importance of effective and efficient productive language treatment procedures for overcoming developmental delays.

HOW TO DETERMINE WHERE TO START

It is important to emphasize that the starting point in this program to facilitate speaking depends on the individual child; therefore, it varies among children. A child with a vocabulary of 20 words and no two-word phrases will begin at a different point than the child with a vocabulary of 70 words and several two-word phrases. In the less sophisticated case, it is necessary to build a disposition to willingly use the words that are already present in the child's vocabulary before trying to increase vocabulary size. It is important to show the child how to use words to communicate and that words have meanings that eventually make communication easier than nonverbal behaviors. In the more language sophisticated child, it would be more appropriate to begin the sessions by increasing the number of two-word productions. Here the child's store of single words is large enough to move on to the next level of language development involving the combination of words into short phrases. Of course, the introduction of new words into the vocabulary is also helpful, but this should be relatively easy; the more difficult task is to increase the number of two-word sentences. The emphasis throughout the program is on encouraging the child through the use of contingent rewards to move to the next higher level of language production.

One fundamental assumption of this program is that the more children use words, the more rapidly they will acquire other productive language skills. Keep in mind that the child is viewed as an active participant in the acquisition of talking. By encouraging this active participation, not only will language learning advance, but it appears that as children's disposition to speak increases, they are more likely to engage in vocal play and to overcome temporary productive-language delays.

In selecting the appropriate starting point, it is important to avoid asking for more than your child is developmentally capable of producing. However, it is of equal importance to avoid underestimating your child's current language potential and, by so doing, expose your child unnecessarily to boring, repetitive drill. Your child's interest and enjoyment are essential features of this program.

The use of the Spontaneous Speech and Receptive Language Record in Table 5.1 provides a means of estimating your child's current productive vocabulary (the number of different words spoken) as well as the size of his or her receptive vocabulary (the number of words that your child understands but does not say). The number and type of different sounds are also recorded for those children who have small vocabularies. In addition, the inventory samples your child's use of multiple-word phrases and his or her understanding of simple requests. The language inventory is not intended to replace a thorough speech and language evaluation, but it does provide a reasonable estimate of your child's current language status particularly if he or she has a small spoken vocabulary. Of equal importance, this estimate of spoken and understood vocabulary helps to identify an appropriate point of entry for this language stimulation program.

ALLOCATION OF TIME

This program is designed to produce measurable improvements in your child's ability to talk, with efficient use of your time over a relatively short period. Our experience has been that depending on the individual child and circumstances, the program may require between 6 and 12 months of effort. Although 12 minutes a day may seem like a relatively short time, in fact, even 12 minutes combined with preparation time and consistency over days amounts to a sizable commitment. Thus, it is important that you, as a parent, appreciate the fact that your role as teacher will not be a trivial investment of time and energy.

Parents of children with delayed speech are often discouraged because past efforts, even prior attempts at rewarding speech, have failed to produce measurable progress. We have found that these efforts have frequently been short lived and often inconsistent from day to day. Consistency in treatment is an essential aspect of this program. It is necessary to conduct the 12-minute sessions at least 5 days each week. Moreover, in the beginning, it is advisable for parents to allow a 4-week trial period for initial progress to occur. It is also desirable to conduct the 12-minute sessions on a daily basis during this initial period. Thus, the brevity of the sessions is compensated for by their consistency over days and weeks.

The consistency of commitment over time provides parents with a distinct advantage—the opportunity to implement a long-range plan. It is important to emphasize that no matter how resistant, noncompliant, or "difficult" a child may be, the adult has a major advantage for changing the child's behavior. The resistant child can only respond to a specific situation at a given moment and does not have a long-range plan that dictates which action should be taken tomorrow or next week. This productive language program provides parents with a plan and a clear advantage for success. As a parent, you can use a strategy that will eventually lead to your child's compliance. In contrast, your child's behavior is characterized by resistance to specific situations without a long-range goal. Your commitment to this project must be sufficient in time to permit the implementation of a long-range plan to change your child's behavior. The tendency for compliance increases as a result of the number of situations in which your child's compliant behavior is followed by reward. If edibles and praise are used as rewards, your child is likely to become less resistant and eventually will produce sounds and words when they are requested. In addition, if rewards are given for compliance in a number of different situations, a general inclination toward compliance will develop. When your child is willing to produce words for rewards, you will gain a powerful method for changing your child's behavior in line with the plan to produce speech. It is the combination of the use of contingent rewards with a plan for promoting the acquisition of talking based on the normal course of language development that forms the foundation of this manual. It is important to recognize that once the ability to talk is acquired, it serves as its own reward; it will not be necessary to use edibles or even praise for very long. In fact, time must be allocated for the elimination of edibles from the sessions. As your child becomes more fluent, the need for extraneous rewards will be diminished systematically. Talking for its own expressed objectives such as a desired object or the communication of a thought must be encouraged. However, 6–12 months may be needed to complete these objectives.

You will know that the end point of this program is approaching when your child displays the ability to communicate complex thoughts and actions using his or her own spontaneously produced multiple-word sentences. This achievement indicating the child's comprehension of his or her mother's request and his or her own spontaneously created appropriate reply was illustrated nicely by one of the first children with whom this manual was developed. In an exasperated response to her mother's request to say, "More candy, please," this child blurted out, "Mommy, give me it." The response clearly indicates that this child was not limited to rote reproductions of her mother's speech. Indeed, she not only fully comprehended what her mother was saying, but was able to process that information and generate her own appropriate response to communicate her strong feelings and thoughts about the request. Similar cogently stated responses are not possible using nonverbal means.

As in this example, the ability to communicate verbally using multiple-word sentences reflects a new and rewarding aspect of this child's world. Edible rewards are extremely helpful in getting this process started and in eliminating noncompliant behaviors that interfere with language acquisition. However, in the final analysis, it is the internal satisfaction that comes from speaking in multiple word sentences that provides the ultimate reward for your child and for you as a parent. Your child's achievement of this milestone will announce that he or she has approached graduation day.

2

The Nature of Noncompliant and Resistant Behavior

INTRODUCTION

The material discussed in this chapter was prepared for use with children who not only have productive-language delays, but who are also difficult and noncompliant when asked to speak. Not all children willingly respond to suggestions to produce sounds or words, not even when incentives such as candies or toys are used to entice them. In fact, some children behave as though they will not talk, no matter what you do. If your child is highly resistant to requests for speech and often does not do what you ask, then it is likely that this chapter will be useful—even necessary—for you. On the other hand, not all children with productive-language delays are strongly resistant or noncompliant. If your child produces words when you request them, then you can probably skip this chapter. If your child is neither clearly resistant nor clearly compliant, the decision about whether you will need the procedures described in this chapter is more difficult. If you are in doubt, perhaps you should read this chapter anyway and decide later whether you need to use these procedures.

Resistant and noncompliant behaviors are discussed here because they may seriously interfere with attempts to produce talking. In fact, it appears that these behaviors may be the major stumbling block to talking for more children with language delays than had been previously believed. The creation of clear-cut, effective procedures to reduce resistant and noncompliant behaviors so that a child will be more responsive to efforts to stimulate talking is a central feature of this program. In fact, this effort to produce compliant behavior most clearly distinguishes our program from other approaches. Our experience revealed that in the past, few effective alternatives have been available to parents for treating noncompliant behaviors. The procedures discussed in this chapter to reduce resistance and increase compliance are a central and effective part of this program.

It appears that there is a continuum of resistance. Most 2- to 3-year-old children refuse to comply with some requests some of the time. But other children present more difficult problems, for they refuse to comply with requests most of the time. In many instances, delays with productive language are accompanied by an overall pattern of resistance and noncompliance to many aspects of behavior, not just talking. It is the combination of refusing to comply with most requests and a serious speech delay that makes the creation of specific procedures to address this problem necessary.

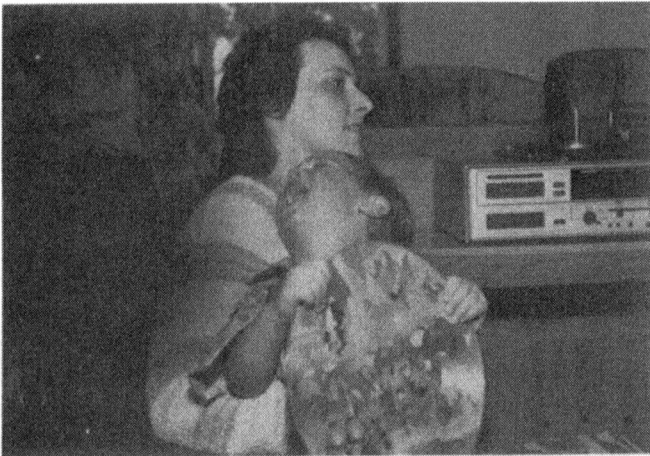

Children may use a variety of behaviors to avoid talking, such as crying, throwing tantrums, silence, and even turning away. Parents often become frustrated in their efforts because it is not possible to encourage speech physically from a child who is unwilling to comply. A resistant child may be physically assisted to bang out a tune on a xylophone, but it is almost impossible to guide the same child physically to say *ball*. Some parents report that their persistent demands to elicit speech often result in mounting levels of resistance by their children, a problem that can be exasperating to parents. In the final analysis, your child must be willing to comply with your requests to produce a word if talking is to occur, whether you use this language stimulation program or not.

If you are a parent of a highly resistant child whose productive language is delayed, do not get discouraged. The procedures to reduce resistance may solve your problem.

AN ILLUSTRATION OF RESISTANT BEHAVIOR

The following attempt to conduct a teaching session using the structured imitation format with a child who was highly resistant illustrates some of the difficulties that may occur in the beginning phases of this program. This mother's requests for talking represented a major change from her previous style of interaction. In the past, she accepted her child's gesturing to communicate because he was generally difficult to control. John would cry, fuss, and have tantrums if his mother insisted that he do as he was told.

Mother:	"Come on, John. Let's try a new word game."
John:	(Shoves the toy truck under the chair.)
Mother:	"John, sit in your chair. I've got some nice things to show you."
John:	"No!"
Mother:	(Picks John up and sits him in the chair.)
John:	(Bangs the table, gets off his chair, runs toward the door yelling.) "No! No!"
Mother:	(Picks up a small ball and follows John around the room.) "John, see the nice ball. Say ball."
John:	(Throws himself on the floor.)
Mother:	(Tries to return him to his chair.)
John:	(Pulls back on the floor and starts kicking and yelling.)
Mother:	"John, stop that! Look at me! Say ball."
John:	(Continues tantrum and bangs his head on the floor.)
Mother:	"John, don't do that." (Picks him up.) "Come on, sit down on the couch and we will read a story. Look at the pictures."
John:	(Stops fussing. Becomes quiet momentarily and sits beside mother, looking at the book. He then pushes her arm away, gets down from the couch, picks up the ball, and throws it across the room.)

This attempted language session was a complete failure. Mother ended the session frustrated, angry, and discouraged. John learned nothing except perhaps that the way to get his mother to show him the picture book is to yell and bang his head on the floor. John's resistance to his mother's requests for sitting quietly and repeating her words is likely to continue. Initially, John must learn to become more compliant and willing to follow his mother's suggestions. Occasionally, as in John's case, it is necessary to introduce compliance activities before, or along with, the productive language sessions.

WHAT ARE THE CONSEQUENCES
OF NONCOMPLIANT AND RESISTANT BEHAVIOR?

Why is it important to identify and minimize noncompliant and resistant behaviors in children? One obvious answer is that the tendency to resist instruction removes a child from many positive learning situations. The child who tends to turn away each time a request is made is at a marked disadvantage relative to children who are cooperative in learning situations. A tendency to resist or be noncompliant to parental requests, instructions, or demands is a serious learning handicap. All too often, resistant children's first reaction is to turn away when their parents introduce something new. The same children may run to the new activity eagerly when their mother leaves the situation. Unfortunately, these children will have lost the benefit of explanation or demonstration by their mother—a vital resource for new learning. What these children gain from the situation when left to their own means, without mother's help, is likely to be less sophisticated than if they allowed her to help.

In many cases, initial resistant and avoidant reactions prevent children from learning more sophisticated uses for toys. We have seen many instances in which developmentally delayed children, who are capable of using objects appropriately, resist instruction by their parents. These same children often resort to less mature forms of play, such as mouthing and banging when left to explore the same toy on their own. For example, they may bang or mouth a toy telephone rather than dial it and put the receiver to their ear, even though they have the necessary intellectual ability to learn to use the objects appropriately. We have shown in our own research that there are advantages to children's intellectual development when they are encouraged to progress from simply mouthing and banging objects to displaying appropriate uses for them. Appropriate uses for objects represent a more advanced form of play than mouthing and banging and set the stage for even more sophisticated pretend games.

In addition to restricting available sources of new information for children, a tendency to resist parental instruction also prevents rehearsal of new information and skills. Without some rehearsal, the newly learned information may not become solidified in a child's repertoire. Even if children were to learn some of the information despite the resistance, it is likely that they would have a poorer memory and less consistency in the use of the new skill. The tendency to resist a parent's further attempts to request and demonstrate the same act may prevent rehearsal or practice of the new information or emerging skill. For example, a neighbor's son, Tommy, who is a resistant child, heard the word *dog* spoken and even attempted an approximation *(duh)* on his own, but refused to speak the sound at his mother's request. The opportunity to strengthen the association between the sound *duh* and the neighbor's dog was decreased. It was not because Tommy was unable to learn or speak, but rather because his immediate reaction to his mother's request to repeat the sound was to resist. It is not that Tommy could not say the word; it is that he could not comply easily. It is not that Tommy lacked the ability; it is that he has learned to resist. The procedures described in the remainder of this chapter were designed to overcome these unfortunate consequences for development associated with resistant behaviors.

There is a second undesirable condition that is the result of resistant behavior. When children do not talk and resist efforts to teach them, the pressure to adjust and learn how to communicate is placed unintentionally on the parents rather than the children. Usually, parents of speech-delayed children have to learn what their child's gestures and grunts mean. Perhaps you have told your own friends that when your child bangs on the refrigerator it means that he or she wants a drink or that standing next to the front door and screaming is what your child does when he or she wants to go out. Communication occurs, but it is nonverbal, and you rather than your child may have been forced to learn the language. Obviously, it is better for your child's development if he or she is taught how to speak instead.

If a language-delayed child merely points and grunts to communicate a thought, the effort is usually unclear and nonspecific. Pointing and grunting indicate simply that the child "wants something." The burden of specificity rests with you, the parent, who must "figure out" exactly what your child really wants. Some parents may offer a child several alternatives to choose from. The effort may be well intentioned, but the need to provide your child a choice each time does not help your child's growth as much as talking would. Nature has arranged the course of development in such a way that learning to talk requires the active participation of each child. Parents and siblings cannot talk for them. The procedures in this manual will help you to assist your child's language development by creating conditions that will maximize the chances that efforts to talk and compliance with requests for speech will occur.

One way to illustrate how undesirable resistant behavior is for a child's development is to contrast it with a compliant style of behavior. When a request is made by a parent, resistant children's first reaction is to remove themselves from the task almost automatically. Resistant or noncompliant children may become unpleasant, negative, and irritable if the request is repeated. The information that the parent is trying to communicate is not likely to penetrate such children's barrage of resistant and inattentive behaviors such as crying, playing with other toys, or pulling away. In time, resistance and noncompliance may lead to incompetence. As the children's avoidance of new material reduces the opportunities to master new skills, they may fall further behind other children. In addition, the successes that children need to gain confidence will be fewer and the children will be less prepared for the many developmental tasks that lie ahead.

With fewer successes, resistant and noncompliant children will have less opportunity to gain praise and rewards for their accomplishments. Indeed, if parents reward resistance, noncompliance, or a child's nonverbal demands, they unknowingly would be strengthening the child's resistance and reducing the chance that it will get turned around. Generally, it is a serious mistake to provide attention, praise, or tangible rewards for resistant and noncompliant behaviors. In short, the combination of a speech delay and resistant behavior is a potentially serious problem that may lead to a host of undesirable behaviors and reduce opportunities for enjoyable consequences. It is equally unfortunate that resistant children may become a source of frustration, displeasure, failure, and even anger for their parents, friends, relatives and teachers. Despite their love for the child, these parents are often denied satisfaction from the child's behavior and have fewer opportunities to enjoy the rewards that children give us. Resistant children are simply more difficult to bring up.

In contrast to the resistant child, compliant children are more likely to be a source of pleasure, achievement, and pride for their parents and teachers. Compliance reflects an openness to learning—a willingness to meet the demands of a new situation. When presented with new information and instruction, compliant children stay with the task, learn it, and express pleasure and delight with their new competence. Children who follow requests are even willing to rehearse the new skills and gain an opportunity to cement it into their repertoire. Because compliant children have a style of interaction that is likely to lead to competence, they elicit praise and rewards that produce positive associations to learning situations and parental requests. Without a doubt, the contrast in consequences for compliant and resistant tendencies during the toddler period is great. Thus, it appears that a child's willingness to cooperate with parental requests during the second and third years of life is associated with clear advantages for that child's development.

PROBLEMS WITH NONVERBAL COMMUNICATION

Before describing the details of the language teaching session and the process of teaching single words to children, particularly speech-delayed children, it is helpful to view productive-language delays in a broad behavioral context. Talking is only one of several avenues of communication available to young children. It is important to realize that gesturing, pointing, grunting, screaming, head banging, or other nonverbal behaviors also convey messages for children. In addition, it is important to recognize that children do not know that there are severe limits to some of these nonverbal forms of communication. They do not know that spoken language is a far more flexible medium for communication than gesturing and that talking paves the way for a more sophisticated level of behavior. Children do not know that their own development will improve if they talk and gesture rather than gesture alone. Young children do not realize that reading, writing, and mathematical ability will be required of them in a few years and that without age-appropriate productive language these developments are in jeopardy.

Conventional tests of mental development rely heavily on both receptive and productive language (what your child understands and says), gross and fine motor development (largely through imitative behaviors), and compliance with the examiner administering the test. Productive language items appear with greater frequency toward the end of the second year, and the ability to speak plays a dominant role in most tests by the third year of life. Thus, children who display delays in any of these areas are likely to fail items on IQ tests and tests of mental development and these lowered estimates of their intellectual ability may place them at risk for mental retardation.

Virtually without exception, the developmentally delayed children that we studied were slow to talk. In addition, the majority of these children had resistant and noncompliant behaviors that required the use of the procedures described in this chapter.

Children with productive-language delays are not aware of the degree to which most nonverbal means of communication tend to limit their social world. Children who point or grunt to indicate their likes and scream and tantrum to indicate their dislikes may be tolerated by parents, but neighbors and friends soon tend to avoid them. Even parents become annoyed and frustrated with children who say a word spontaneously one moment and refuse steadfastly to repeat the same word 10 seconds later. The behavior of speech-delayed children may gradually isolate them from other people and the naturally occurring social experiences that are necessary for normal social development.

The children for whom this manual is intended are intellectually and physically able to speak. Unfortunately, their delay in talking is often worsened by learning an alternate and temporarily successful form of communication. Thus, it is usually the case that language-delayed children must "unlearn" the old often incompatible form of communication before they learn to make their needs known by talking. It is not easy to break habits, as we have said before. Much of the resistance that may be encountered in fostering productive language stems from the child's unwillingness to abandon a temporarily effective form of nonverbal communication in favor of speech. Young children have no understanding of these alternatives. It is our responsibility as parents and professionals to help these children out of the blind alley created by these alternate forms of communication.

There are many instances of resistant behavior among 2- and 3-year-old children that fall within normal limits. A child's resistance to change occurs as a matter of degree. One child may be highly resistant in many areas relative to another child who may be highly compliant. Still another child may be resistant in some situations only. As children enter the middle of the second year, many new demands are imposed on them. For example, children are expected to walk rather than be carried, to use the toilet rather than soil themselves, and to drink from a cup rather than a bottle. They are asked to share toys with their brothers and sisters, to "be nice" to the baby, and to avoid screaming when they want something. They are presented with many new restrictions. They are told for the first time that they cannot touch daddy's books, that they must keep out of mommy's cosmetics, and that they must not touch grandmother's china dish.

From the children's point of view, these new demands reflect a marked change in their social environment. The fact that many children typically do not take these new demands lightly is borne out by the label that we have attached to this period—"the terrible 2s." Almost all children show some resistance to some of these new demands some of the time. This reluctance to conform to some of these new restrictions can be regarded as a normal degree of resistance. The difficulty arises when this normally occurring resistance becomes excessive and linked to an important aspect of development such as talking.

RESISTANCE TO CHANGE

Often, when speech-delayed children are asked to give up an effective nonverbal means of communication such as gesturing alone, they protest. Children do not know that there is a limit to what can be communicated effectively through pointing, gesturing, and grunting. They also do not realize how important talking is for further development or how much the adult world uses productive language to judge their mental ability formally and informally. Both parents and professionals have to make these decisions for children.

Children who resist attempts to substitute one set of well-learned behaviors for another are not unlike adults. Many adults trying to "cut back" on smoking would express anger or resentment if another adult removed their cigarettes. Similarly, many dieters would protest if another person attempted to restrict their caloric intake. Most of us would prefer to change our own behavior and develop our own plan. Unfortunately, 2-year-old children do not have the capacity to develop their own plan. We as parents and professionals have to develop their plan for them. This long-term planning is a large part of what we mean when we refer to parental responsibilities for child rearing. As parents, we make decisions for our children that are in their best interest. Thus, if your child resists the implementation of the program to encourage talking, do not view it as a hostile act. Your child's protest is both part of the problem and an expected outcome. Do not be surprised if some protest occurs.

Resistant children are not bad; they are simply resisting change, just as adults resist change even when the change is in their best interest. The resistance is not directed at the adult per se. The child's resistance occurs because the adult is tampering with a habit that has been successful. It is essential to keep in mind that your child's resistance is a byproduct of his or her habits and not an expression of dislike for you as a parent. This point should be repeated: Resistant children are not bad children and should not be treated as offenders. They need help and understanding.

WHEN IS A TODDLER OVERLY RESISTANT?

Resistance is most clearly identified in a particular child when a request is made for the child to produce a known, well-learned behavior. For example, a child may know how to say *ball,* but refuse when asked to do so and display one or more of a variety of resistant behaviors. The reaction is frequently clear when an extremely resistant child is asked to do something that he may not wish to do. For example, a young boy may scream, fight, hit his parents, throw himself on the floor, bang his head, and have a full blown temper tantrum when told he cannot have his juice unless he says *juh.* But in its more subtle forms, resistance, particularly to requests for speech, is difficult to identify. A child's behavior may look more like noncompliance than active resistance. A mildly resistant young girl may simply avoid looking at her mother, turn her attention to another object, remain blank as though she did not comprehend the question, or give the impression that she is tired. She may engage in a distracting activity that may successfully deflect her mother's attention. She may bang her hand on a table repetitively when told to remain seated until dinner is finished. More subtly, when asked to get a book, she may pick up another object while smiling and laughing. If you are sure that your child can perform a certain act, but if he or she displays one or more of these evasive behaviors instead in several situations, then it is likely that your child is overly resistant.

The results from our own longitudinal investigation of children with developmental delays revealed a strong association between productive-language delays and resistant behavior. Of the 44 children enrolled in the study with clear delays on the Bayley Scale of Mental Development, 33 (77%) displayed clear evidence of resistance in a standardized observational situation. Noncompliant and resistant behavior was tested by asking parents to teach their children the uses for three different toys—a telephone, xylophone, and puzzle. Children who were resistant responded to their parents with physical and verbal behaviors that indicated refusal. For example, when asked to play with one of the toys, the more resistant children tended to push the toy away, struggle, kick, and pull away from their parents or throw the toys around. Children who were non-compliant responded to their parents with behaviors that indicated avoidance. They simply played with another toy, or if they could speak, said *home* or some other word that reflected their desire to leave the situation. The same situation produced appropriate play and compliance from most children whose behavior was developing normally.

Fortunately, noncompliant and resistant behavior can be changed. It is a behavior that has been "learned" or acquired and as such can be "unlearned." The procedures described in this chapter are designed to free your child from some of the difficulties that may develop along with noncompliant and resistant behaviors. In the majority of cases, the advantages to be gained by children and their parents from overcoming resistance to talking greatly outweigh the inconvenience and effort that must be put in.

HOW MAY RESISTANT BEHAVIOR START?
WHY MAY IT PERSIST?

We have indicated that the tendency either to comply or resist instruction differs markedly from one child to the next. One important point to recognize is that the tendency either to comply or resist is acquired and, therefore, can be changed. Compliance and resistance can be increased or decreased in children. Consider what would happen if a child's compliance to a request were met with frowning and turning away by the adult. Chances are that the child would be less and less inclined to do what was asked. Why would the child persist if his or her compliance elicited silence and the withdrawal of attention? On the other hand, consider what would happen if compliance to an adult's requests were met with hugs, kisses, and expressions of delight. There is little doubt that the child would be more likely to comply with future requests. It is a strong law of behavior that following a desired response with a reward increases the chance that the response will occur again. The responses that we want to increase are compliance and talking.

Resistant behavior, like compliant behavior, can be changed by the consequences produced in a child's social world. If every instance of resistance or noncompliance were met with silence and the withdrawal of attention, the child's resistance would decline because it would cease to be successful behavior. It takes time, practice, and patience for both children and adults to learn new behaviors, particularly if old and established competing behaviors must be unlearned. Stated simply, those behaviors that satisfy childrens' needs and result in praise from their parents and friends become part of their day-to-day behavioral repertoire. Behaviors that do not earn a good return and fail to attract the attention and praise of adults gradually disappear.

If resistant behaviors start and persist, it is because they continue to satisfy a child's needs and are supported by the child's social environment, almost always unintentionally. At this point, it is important for you to examine the consequences that are provided to your child's resistant behavior. It is sometimes difficult but necessary to face the fact that your child's undesirable behavior may be unintentionally rewarded at home. If you have been forced to give in when your child resists your demands, there is a good chance that you will be able to change that situation.

3 Reversing Noncompliant Behaviors

INTRODUCTION

It is not enough to be able to identify an overly resistant language-delayed child, but identification is a necessary first step. In this chapter, we describe procedures to reduce resistant and noncompliant behaviors effectively. Unfortunately, it is not enough simply to eliminate these behaviors, but elimination is a necessary second step. Thus, effective procedures to promote compliance are also presented, and these compliance activities represent a positive third step toward restoring a behavioral readiness for talking. The compliance activities create a behavioral receptivity for imitative and spontaneous speech where resistance may have occurred previously.

HOW CAN RESISTANCE BE REVERSED?

Reducing resistant behaviors in your child requires that you use two strategies simultaneously. First, all supports and unintentional rewards for resistant behavior must be eliminated. As we have said before, if the resistant behavior becomes unsuccessful, it will diminish. For example, a child may scream when his mother insists that he talk. If this child is placed in a corner until he stops, rather than picked up and quieted as his mother used to do, screaming will gradually disappear. Second, if resistant behaviors are to be reduced, alternative behaviors that you want your child to display must be identified, demonstrated, and rewarded. For example, talking may be identified as a more desirable behavior than screaming. The language training sessions will be used to model, elicit, and reward the use of specific words for your child. Gradually, your child's resistance to your demands for speech will decrease as he or she gains more words. As this happens, the frustration produced by the inability to talk in the first place will be eliminated.

If a child is to learn to use words to communicate his or her needs, gesturing alone and crying must stop producing positive results. Nonverbal behaviors alone cannot continue to be effective. Thus, the first part of the two-part strategy to lessen resistance is to reduce the undesired behavior. It should be clear that the elimination of crying and tantrums will not be enough to produce talking, in itself. It is also necessary to isolate and model the behavior that is desired (talking, in this case) and to specifically reward approximations to the proper words for the objects that the child may desire. In the beginning, it is better for children to say *muh* for milk than to allow them to enter the refrigerator and take the milk on their own. The poorly articulated, "almost correct" word *muh* is preferred because it literally reverses the form of communication that the child uses. Shaping compliance to a request to produce a sound or word is an essential part of this two-step process. In the beginning, this change from nonverbal to verbal communication may take time, practice, and persistance. It is also important for you to know that change comes more slowly during the beginning of this program. Further change will occur at an increasingly faster rate as your child begins to improve.

Because the tendency to resist is often rewarded unintentionally, it is frequently difficult for well-meaning parents to recognize resistant behavior. As a result, resistance may be difficult to eliminate initially. Most parents have a strong desire to do what is best for their child and become concerned when developmental difficulties arise. For example, head banging elicits immediate concern from both parents and professionals who justifiably become alarmed and fearful that an injury will occur. The instinctive reaction of most parents is to attend to their child when head banging occurs. They pick up the child and provide comfort and solace. However, each prompt delivery of comfort by the parent strengthens the probability that the child will bang his or her head the next time that frustration or distress occurs. This is an instance when parental instincts, intuition, and genuine concern for the welfare of a child conspire to make the problem worse. The solution is counterintuitive and nonobvious; the parent should walk away from the child (withdraw attention), rather than provide comfort, when head banging occurs. The solution becomes obvious if you ask what the child attempts to achieve by banging his or her head? Most head banging appears to occur when the child is in a frustrating situation and seeks parental comfort or solace as an escape from the stressful event.

Few children bang their head with sufficient force to produce serious injury. In fact, head banging usually produces more anxiety for the parent than pain for the child; therefore, it is a successful behavior for children to use to satisfy their needs. As head banging fails to meet a child's needs, it will gradually disappear—particularly if an alternative acceptable behavior is demonstrated to the child and rewarded when it occurs. The lesson gleaned from this example is that it is necessary for parents to assert control over their child's behavior—to understand what it is that the child is attempting to accomplish and to teach the child a more acceptable means for achieving that goal.

Three techniques can be used to help eliminate unintentional rewards for undesirable behavior in your child. First, you can remove yourself by simply walking away when an unwanted behavior occurs. If you do not provide attention, the behavior will become ineffective and will stop occurring. The reduction of a behavior (e.g., temper tantrums) as a result of its occurrence *without* a reward is a well-established behavioral principle called *extinction*.

A second way to reduce resistant behavior is to remove the activity, rather than yourself, from the child. For example, suppose that your child was playing with a toy, became frustrated, had a temper tantrum, and threw toys around the room. In this case, the toys, rather than your child, can be removed until quiet, positive behaviors occur. Your child's tantrums will have caused the loss of a rewarding activity—the toys.

A third strategy for removing unintentional rewards for undesirable behaviors involves removing your child from the stimulating activity by placing him or her in a corner. In this instance, your child's crying may increase at first, but it will shortly begin to diminish because the corner will become boring. If your child understands much of what you say, then it is appropriate to state that he or she can return to the rest of the family or the center of the activity when quieting occurs. You should return your child to the normal activity of the household if he or she remains quiet for at least 15 seconds, and eventually for as long as 1 or even 2 minutes. We are not suggesting physical punishment in these circumstances, but it is important to let your child know the reason for being placed in the corner. Sometimes a stern voice can be helpful here.

It is also important to tell your child which behavior (quieting, in this case) will restore your good graces. The amount of quiet behavior that you demand need not be great; anywhere from 15 seconds to about 2 minutes is sufficient, but be sure that it occurs. When quieting occurs and your child is return to center stage, demonstrate the kind of behavior that should have taken place. For example, tell your child the word for the object he or she wanted or demonstrate the appropriate use of the toy that may have produced frustration. If your child complies with your request, then it is important to reward your child with praise even if he or she was just reprimanded. In a nutshell, the dual strategy for changing behavior requires that your child be shown a negative result when undesirable behavior occurs and a positive result when desirable behavior happens.

All three strategies just described are based on the assumption that it is necessary to remove the rewards that are supporting an unwanted behavior. If your child's behavior does not achieve its intended objective, it will stop occurring. To summarize, when children engage in any of a wide spectrum of resistant behaviors in order to communicate their needs, it is important that the resistant behavior be unsuccessful.

An excessive reliance on gesturing and resistance to requests for speech often go hand in hand among children with delayed productive language. Gesturing and talking are not incompatible, but there are strong tendencies for both parent and child to rely on gesturing alone among speech-delayed children. If talking is to develop, gesturing *alone* can no longer be successful. Thus, a child should not get picked up for simply raising his or her arms. Instead, the child should be required to make a sound approximating the word *up*, whether the arms are raised or not.

Unlike gesturing and talking, crying and talking are incompatible behaviors. A child cannot talk properly while crying. If crying is the child's substitute for talking, then crying cannot be rewarded; it must be ignored and eliminated. If talking is to develop, the child must make an attempt at a word without crying or having tantrums. Crying cannot be a successful response for getting a toy car back from a brother, for example. The child must stop both the crying and tantrums and ask for the toy by making a sound approximating *car*. Unless the rewards for crying are eliminated, why should this child be expected to make an effort to talk?

Why is it that the elimination of resistant behaviors is not enough in itself to produce talking? The problem with eliminating behaviors alone as a means to change is that it does not produce any new behavior. Removing rewards for undesirable behaviors merely reduces the chance that those behaviors will occur again. It is not enough that children learn only what not to do; they must also learn what to do. The child must be given appropriate behavior for the situation. For example, if crying is ignored, eventually a child will not cry, but talking will not occur automatically. It is necessary to encourage talking if it is to develop.

Our experience indicates that with speech-delayed children, it is necessary to demonstrate, elicit, and reward talking. Most language-delayed children do not yet have sufficient vocabulary to use speech as an alternative to crying. Fortunately, new behaviors are learned effectively through the contingent use of rewards. In other words, it is necessary to follow attempts at talking with positive consequences such as attention, praise, a desired object and edibles if a speech-delayed child is to begin to talk more.

WHEN TO USE SHAPING AND IMITATION

The 12-minute teaching sessions that serve as the "backbone" of this productive language stimulation program can take at least two different forms. In one form (known as "shaping"), the teaching session can have the appearance of a relaxed interaction with you and your child on the floor playing with one or two toys. Your child may be free to roam, and you may suggest words by naming and presenting toys. However, in this case, you should reward whatever words your child may use whether they were asked for or not. For example, if you ask your child to say the word *car* and he or she picks up a ball and names it, your child should be rewarded for saying *ball*. In another form of the teaching session (known as "imitation"), you and your child may be seated opposite each other at a small table, giving the interaction a more structured appearance. You may direct your child's attention to a particular object such as a ball and request that he or she repeat the word *ball*. In this case, if you are asking your child to imitate you, only your child's use of the modeled word *ball* should be rewarded.

Both procedures are useful and effective and increase production, but they achieve slightly different styles of talking. Whether one or the other is appropriate for a particular child is discussed later. At this point in the program, it is enough to point out that in the more structured imitation situation, you must have greater control over your child's speech and behavior generally. A more sophisticated level of talking can usually be encouraged when using the structured imitation situation in the early phases of the program. The behavioral demands are generally greater also. Your child must be willing to remain seated for a period of time, attend to your actions, and respond to a series of requests for specific words. In the imitation sessions, it is necessary for your child to be compliant and cooperative if the sessions are to be successful. Many children are not ready for this more productive and efficient teaching situation when they begin this program. That is the main reason why it is sometimes necessary to use the shaping procedure to encourage talking and compliant behavior.

SHAPING MOTOR ACTIONS AND WORDS TO PRODUCE COMPLIANCE

If a child is compliant, he or she cannot be resistant. These are incompatible behaviors. The process of shaping compliant behavior works because it is a positive and rewarding experience for your child. A more compliant child will be the well-deserved reward of your efforts. To shape compliance it is advisable to set aside 10–15 minutes each day during which requests can be made and your child's compliance with those requests can be rewarded. By rewarding compliant behavior when it occurs, you will increase the chance that it will occur again. This knowledge allows for simple, even incidental, requests for compliance to grow into more complex and explicit demands. Compliance for requests to perform simple motor actions can develop into compliance with complex speech acts. Similarly, compliance on tasks that your child enjoys will grow naturally into compliance on tasks that he or she may dislike initially.

Usually, it is easier to get a language-delayed child to perform simple motor actions than to speak on command. If your child is highly resistant to requests for speech, begin by shaping compliance to motor actions. There are advantages to accepting compliance to motor actions in the beginning. One of the most important advantages is that an otherwise unpleasant situation may be changed into a pleasant one. For example, in the beginning it is sometimes desirable to ask children to point to their nose, touch their hair, point to mommy's ear, clap their hands, and throw a ball. By rewarding each of these actions, you may gain control of the interaction and be better able to direct your child. Even though your child may be performing an activity that he or she enjoys, it is also being done at your request. Even these small acts of compliance can represent an important turnaround in your child, because resistant children often engage in activities only when they choose. In effect, they control many situations through resistant behavior. If you are to be successful in teaching your child how to use words to communicate, it is essential that you be the teacher and your child the student. To do so, you must be able to get your child to follow your requests.

This manual provides you with a clear advantage in your bid for control. Generally, young children respond to situations in terms of the positive and negative consequences that are provided. They do things that are rewarded and avoid activities that are ineffective or strongly punished. Young children do not have plans for each situation. On the other hand, the productive language training program provides you with a clear plan and the leverage necessary to change your child's behavior. The control you gain from shaping motor actions will help you to carry out the plan contained in this manual. In addition, by encouraging compliance to simple motor actions, your rewards and praise can change an interaction from a negative and resistant experience to a positive one. Furthermore, by rewarding compliance to motor actions that your child will perform easily, he or she can gain a sense of satisfaction and develop competence on a small scale.

Motor activities more sophisticated than clapping hands should be used if your child is cognitively advanced. If he or she is 30 months of age or older and intellectually normal, simple practical life tasks will probably be of greater interest and more likely to elicit compliance. A series of simple household chores may be more appropriate to assign and reward. For example, your child could be asked to put the trash in the wastebasket, place clothes in a hamper, bring the paper to daddy, place the dishes on the table, or pick up the toys and place them on the shelf. Physical exercises such as stretching arms upward, touching toes, running in place, and deep knee bends done in imitation of a model and on command might also be of interest to a child whose development is more sophisticated, but is resistant nonetheless. Games like Simon Says are fun and at the same time reduce the tendency to resist simple requests. However, as with the practical life tasks, it is important to provide explicit rewards in the form of praise and edibles for each successful act of compliance.

It is also important to repeat the activities consistently on a daily basis. Consistency cannot be overemphasized with 2- to 3-year-old children. An undesirable and possibly resistance-producing situation can be turned into a positive event if treated with consistency because repetition makes an unfamiliar event become familiar. With familiarity, both the likelihood of success and the number of rewards will rise and the sessions will become increasingly more pleasant. It is the creation of pleasantness and competence in your child that will result in a greater willingness to comply with your requests.

Increasingly, your child's new tendency to comply can begin to influence the language training sessions. Because talking is a more difficult task for a language-delayed child than performing a gross motor act, it is generally more likely to elicit resistance. It is important to keep in mind that the primary reason for including compliance activities is to produce a child who is willing to attempt to make sounds on request during the language training sessions. The child who has learned to comply with requests for motor actions will have learned the game of "give-and-take" that appears necessary for the development of normal verbal interaction. The language shaping and motor compliance sessions can teach your child that he or she must give a little to get a little, and they may teach you that by giving a little to your child you can get a lot of success in return. Thus, in the beginning when it is needed, compliance to motor activities should be encouraged on a regular basis in addition to the language sessions. Although only 12-minute sessions are needed, they should be done at least 5 days each week.

CHOOSING A FORMAT FOR TRAINING COMPLIANCE

As we have said earlier, there are at least two formats for both the compliance and language training sessions. One is more structured and formal in appearance than the other. The structured version requires that your child be seated in a chair and not allowed to wander, as demonstrated in the previous example. In this format, it is necessary for your child to follow your instructions, whether the emphasis is on compliance or language activities. For example, compliance can be encouraged by placing your child in a highchair and enticing him or her to stack blocks. Stacking can be demonstrated, and you can even guide your child physically through the act. You may get more resistance in this structured format, but distractions and nonproductive chasing of your child are far less likely to occur.

The second format is less structured in the sense that your child may be allowed to roam on the floor and therefore have greater access to objects in the room. It is important to eliminate as many distractions as possible. For example, the toys that you use should be kept in a bag and brought out one at a time. Because the less structured format allows your child greater mobility, protest is less likely. In some cases, a child who is allowed to roam on the floor will comply enough to allow the parent to reward successes contingently. On the other hand, if you are able to gain only slight control under these circumstances, then perhaps the structured format should be used. The critical factor in either situation is to elicit the compliant behavior that is desired and to follow it with a reward. The two formats differ mostly in the manner used to elicit the desired behavior, but both strategies will lead to talking eventually.

The two formats also lend themselves to slightly different styles of talking. The less structured format is more conducive to shaping than to imitation and may be more appropriate for the highly resistant child who will not imitate but will say words on his or her own. Following this child's words with rewards will eventually lead to control over the child's speech. On the other hand, the structured format can be imposed when the child is willing to imitate. Imitative speech allows new words to be acquired rapidly and although it is not the end point of this program, it is an important step along the way that will allow expansion of the vocabulary in an efficient manner. Thus, the shaping procedure can be used to bring the child up to a level where he or she will begin to imitate adult speech.

The appropriate choice of format for a given child is the result of many considerations, but oddly enough, the choice is often obvious. The less structured format is appropriate if your child will not imitate you, protests vigorously in the formal situation, but shows interest and cooperation in the less structured situation. However, if the less structured situation is unmanageable with your child because he or she becomes frantic or chaotic, you will have no choice but to impose a structured format. If tighter controls are needed, place your child in a highchair or at a table pushed against a wall. In the end, the choice of format that is appropriate for your child is the one that leads to success with the least amount of resistance and difficulty. If in doubt, try each of the formats to determine which is most suitable for your child's style.

AN ILLUSTRATION OF APPROPRIATE
COMPLIANCE TRAINING

Robert is a 32-month-old child with delayed productive language who is also highly resistant to instruction, but manageable in a nonstructured situation. His mother has found that he will comply with tasks that he enjoys, but raises a fuss when she asks him either to say words or follow simple commands. She has also learned to keep the toys that she uses in this "compliance-shaping" situation in a large bag that removes them from sight. She has chosen to use a ball to play with because she knows that Robert enjoys bouncing, rolling, and throwing a ball. By beginning with a task that is enjoyable to Robert, compliance is virtually guaranteed. Robert will throw the ball only because he enjoys throwing it. If his mother suggests that he throw it, he will comply with her suggestion in this instance, because he wishes to throw the ball anyway. Nonetheless, if Robert's mother rewards him with praise and edibles, she will increase the probability that he will comply again. Because he is enjoying himself, Robert may "forget" about his resistance temporarily. His mother may even be able to make other suggestions and gain his compliance for retrieving the ball or perhaps rolling it, for example.

Mother: (Presents the ball to Robert.) "Do you want to throw the
           ball?"
Robert: (Snatches the ball and throws it across the room.)
Mother: "Good boy, Robert. You threw the ball." (Rewards
           Robert with an M & M.)
Robert: (Wanders past mother with the ball in his hand.)
Mother: (Gently removes the ball from Robert's hand.) "Do you
           want to throw the ball again?"
Robert: (Approaches his mother and reaches for the ball.)
Mother: "Here's the ball." (Hands the ball to Robert.)
Robert: (Throws the ball across the room.)
           "Good boy, Robert. You threw the ball. That was a good
           throw." (Places an M & M in Robert's mouth.) "Can you
           get me the ball, Robert?"
Robert: (Immediately goes after the ball, but does not bring it
           directly to mother.)
Mother: "Let's play a different game. Come here and I'll show
           you a different game."
Robert: (Comes to his mother).
Mother: (Gently removes the ball from Robert's hand.) "Sit here
           and I'll roll the ball to you." (Sits Robert down, spreads
           his legs, and rolls the ball to him.)
Robert: (Stops the ball between his legs.)
Mother: "Good boy, Robert. You caught the ball." (Puts an M &
           M in Robert's mouth and sits down herself.) "Now, you
           roll it to me."
Robert: (Stands up and rolls the ball to his mother.)
Mother: "Good job, Robert. You rolled the ball to me. This is a
           great game." (Places another M & M in Robert's mouth
           as he approaches her.)

This compliance session between Robert and his mother contains several important lessons. First, Robert's mother knows that Robert is more likely to do what she asks if she makes her requests indirectly. Suggestions rather than demands appear to be more successful with him. Second, she has also learned in the past that she can get Robert to play more if she takes the initiative to encourage him, so she directs the activity. She uses her plan to elicit compliance. In time, Robert's mother will be able to make more direct requests and demands of Robert and still get him to comply. Third, Robert's mother gave the M & M's to him in an incidental manner. She never even mentioned the candy, only the task at hand. Fourth, Robert's mother changed the objectives slightly during the game so that she could maintain his interest. She started with throwing and changed to rolling the ball. Fifth,Robert's mother withheld the ball until she was prepared to make a new request. She controlled the interaction by holding the ball until Robert complied with her requests. Giving him the ball when he followed her suggestions was a good example of contingent reward of compliant behavior.

Each time Robert complied with his mother's suggestions, his resistance was lessened by a small amount. In addition, he gained an appreciation for his mother's praise and the M & M's that she gave him. Robert's desire for his mother's praise is an important lever that all parents have for helping their children. Contingent parental praise and approval is the primary source of power used in these compliance and language training sessions. It is necessary to be aware of that fact to use it most effectively.

As a parent, you should recognize that your child cares much more about your attention and praise than anyone else's. It matters to your child when you praise and reward him or her. It also matters if you withdraw your attention when your child is misbehaving. Unfortunately, reasoning is often not enough to get a highly resistant child to do what you want, so do not be afraid to use contingent rewards. They represent a powerful tool that parents can use to lead their language-delayed children back on to the course of normal development.

GENERALIZATION OF COMPLIANCE
TO MANY TASKS: AN ILLUSTRATION

Obviously, it is not enough to let children perform only those tasks that they enjoy, although enjoyable tasks provide a good starting point. It is necessary to move constantly to slightly more difficult demands. In Robert's case, his mother may ask him to put some clothes in the hamper. At first he may not understand the request, and it may be necessary to show him. His mother could help him understand what she means by demonstrating the act or even by guiding him through each step. She could hold Robert's hand while he clutched a towel and walk with him to the hamper. She could allow him to drop the towel into the hamper and then reward him with praise and a treat. She would be wise to allow Robert the pleasure of the final step in this sequence—the chance to drop the towel into the hamper. With that, Robert's mother should say, "Good boy, Robert. You just put the towel in the hamper for mommy," and then place an M & M in his mouth. Each time that she helped him, she should provide less physical assistance. For example, the second time that she told him to bring a towel to the hamper, Robert should be made to carry the towel himself. His mother could simply walk with him to be sure that his mind stayed on the task. When they reached the hamper, she could open it for him and allow him to put the towel in on his own. Again, his successful completion of the task should be followed by praise and a treat. During other sessions, Robert's mother could provide less and less assistance until Robert would simply place the clothes in the hamper when she asked him.

One reason it may be easier to get a child to complete a motor task is because children can be helped physically to perform the task. Robert's mother was able to hold the towel with him and keep him to the task until the towel was dropped into the hamper. This physcial guidance cannot be done with talking. Robert's mother cannot help Robert sound out a word except by following his "almost correct" words with rewards. In this sense, talking requires more of the child's cooperation than physical actions. You cannot produce a sound for your child in the same way that you can physically guide your child through a motor sequence. As a result, motor tasks are an important avenue through which compliance can be fostered.

However, motor tasks in themselves do not help produce talking directly. It is the tendency to comply with requests that help to elicit talking. Therefore, it is important to create about six to ten tasks that your child will comply with so that he or she can acquire a general tendency to comply with your wishes. One or two tasks alone may not be sufficient to foster a compliant tendency. However, six to ten varied tasks will give your child enough opportunity to learn that compliance brings rewards. With a greater tendency to comply rather than resist, your child may become more willing to attempt sounds and words when you request them during the language training sessions.

THE RELATION BETWEEN COMPLIANCE ACTIVITIES
AND THE SPEECH SESSIONS

The control of resistant behavior has been emphasized thus far because resistance is often an overriding factor that interferes with a child's development in general and with the language teaching sessions in particular. The strategies that we have suggested to reduce resistant behavior should be carried out in addition to the language training sessions. The primary reason for the compliance activities is to help your child gain a tendency to use words for communication. As a tendency to be more cooperative develops, your child will be more willing to attempt the sounds or say the words that you request during the language training sessions. The important point to remember is that talking is our primary goal, but often, sounds and words cannot be elicited if your child resists your efforts almost automatically.

Not all children are so resistant as to require special sessions aimed solely at reducing noncompliant behavior, but some are. In these cases, progress with talking may depend on producing more compliant behavior. However, most children at one time or another during the course of their language training sessions will refuse to comply with requests for words, especially when new and difficult words are introduced. Words with more than one syllable, two- and three-word combinations, and certain sound combinations are more difficult to say than others and may lead to temporary resistance when introduced. In addition, words that your child may not understand—abstract concepts, prepositions, and conjuctions such as under, over, but, and if—may produce resistance because they are difficult. It is at these times that techniques for dealing with resistance may be helpful to all parents using the manual.

CONCLUDING COMMENTS

You should approach the teaching sessions believing that your child will cooperate. If your child displays resistance instead, then you should be prepared to deal with it. However, if your child is compliant, then you have gained a major advantage in your effort to help your child speak. With the reduction of resistance, your child's language training program will have moved ahead in an important way.

Most resistance will diminish if dealt with consistently and firmly in the way that we have described. However, during your first attempts, resistance may actually increase. You should be prepared to wait out the situation if resistance appears to be worsening during your initial attempts. It may be that you have learned to avoid making demands upon your child in the past. If nearly every request resulted in a struggle, it would not take long to learn to avoid requests and to "work around" a resistant child. Initially, your child may protest any change in the way that you interact with him or her. If your child knows that he can get what he wants by having a 2-minute tantrum, the tantrum may increase to 5 or 10 minutes the first time that you choose to walk away from it. Do not become alarmed; you have chosen the right course. Once it is clear to your child that tantrums will no longer work, the tantrums will gradually diminish. Both the frequency and the intensity with which they occur will decrease. The gradual decline will be an indication that your child is beginning to learn that his or her needs will not be satisfied by resistant behavior.

The decline in your child's resistant behavior is likely to be gradual. That is why you should look for small changes in the length of each tantrum, the number of tantrums each day, and even the feeling shown during each tantrum. The child who has stopped tantrums for several days has not forgotten how to throw a tantrum and may try it out on occasion, especially when asked to perform more difficult tasks. This reappearance of an "extinguished" (eliminated) behavior is a well-known behavioral principle called *spontaneous recovery*. The reappearance of resistance does not mean that all your previous efforts have failed. On the contrary, you will find that eliminating tantrums a second or third time is far easier than it was the first time. Tantrums will be less intense, less prolonged, less frequent, and they will diminish more rapidly each time you have to deal with them. Each time, your child will have learned a little more about the ineffectiveness of tantrums. However, your child may need reminding from time to time. You should be prepared to deal with the reappearance of tantrums or other noncompliant behaviors with the same consistent, nonrewarding approach that you used to eliminate them in the beginning. The reappearance of tantrums is expected, and if dealt with effectively each time, the experience will teach your child more convincingly that it is a behavior that will no longer work.

We have already mentioned that resistance can take many forms. Tantrums, screaming, and head banging are extreme examples. However, quiet, passive refusal to do anything but sit in a highchair and stare at you can also be resistant behavior. Quiet refusal may be easier for you to tolerate, but it is still effective for your child. The end result is the same as head banging and screaming. A quietly noncompliant child can refuse to talk just as effectively as a screaming child. Both types of behavior should be treated in the same way. Turning your back on the silent, noncompliant child and removing your attention and rewards can be as effective in overcoming this form of noncompliance as in eliminating more active forms of resistance.

At this point, your child is ready to begin the 12-minute sessions to encourage talking. It is likely that you will need to continue the procedures to reduce resistant behavior and encourage compliance, but now they can be conducted along with the procedures to encourage talking directly. The remainder of this manual describes a course of development from single-word approximations to three- and four-word sentences that are close to what occurs naturally. That similarity is intentional, and we and others have found that there is a strong developmental sequence to the acquisition of language as shown in Table 1.1. The behavioral procedures used during the 12-minute sessions are designed to encourage your child back onto this naturally developing pathway. The language sessions rely completely on your child's active participation and contribution to the development of talking.

4 An Overview of the Language Teaching Sessions

INTRODUCTION

The language teaching sessions are the core of the productive language program. They are important for teaching new words and phrases and for giving a child regular practice in using speech. The teaching sessions are designed to last for only 12 minutes and should be conducted each day for at least 5 days per week. The brevity of the sessions and consistency over days are major advantages of this program. The sessions should be well organized and planned to meet your child's specific language learning needs each day so that they will run smoothly and effectively.

We are often asked why we chose to have the sessions last for 12 minutes. In part, the decision was arbitrary, and 10- or 15-minute sessions could have been chosen just as easily. However, we have found through trial and error that 12 minutes each day is a tolerable amount of time for a child to work in a single session. This relatively small investment of time is sufficient, if repeated consistently over days, to allow the learning to occur at a rate that you can observe easily. The sessions are brief enough so that they do not become burdensome, yet long enough to produce results that you can see in short order. You will see also that the 12-minute session lends itself to a division into a "warm-up phase" during which easy words are rehearsed and rewarded, a "working phase" during which new and more difficult words are introduced, and a final "review phase" during which both old and new easy words are rehearsed so that the sessions may end on a positive note.

The chapters in this manual, beginning with single words on through multiple-word sentences, contain three commmon sections along with other suggestions. Each chapter begins with a description of the teaching sessions and the appropriate goals to be pursued during that session for that level of development. Following this discussion, a list of events and props that can be used during less formal versions of the sessions, particularly as talking progresses, is provided. The events and props that are listed toward the end of the chapter can be used to focus attention on talking during everyday activities. Each chapter concludes with a description of how the newly acquired abilities can be systematically generalized or extended to situations outside the teaching sessions. In general, these activities are designed to immerse your child into a sea of language.

AN ILLUSTRATION

A "typical" language teaching session can illustrate the procedure itself and help to demonstrate the preparation that is needed. Questions can be raised and solutions more effectively explained when a concrete example is presented, hence readers should imagine the following scenario.

It was early in the evening, and David and his mother were sitting at the kitchen table. His father was sitting off to the side with a watch having a second hand, a recording sheet, and pen ready to record David's verbal responses. David's mother was teaching him to name parts of the body. She had a list of the words that she planned to teach resting in front of her on the table. She began the warm-up phase by having David rehearse the names of body parts that he knew well. She continued into the working phase and taught the name of body parts that David did not know well. He was looking at his mother's face.

Mother: (Points to her nose.) "Nose. David, say nose."
David: "Noh."
Mother: "Good, David. You said nose." (Mother smiles and gives David a chocolate chip. Father writes down *noh* during minute 3 on the recording sheet.)
Mother: (Points to her nose again.) "Nose. David, say nose."
David: "Nose."
Mother: "Good,David. You said nose." (Mother smiles and gives David another chocolate chip. This time father writes the word *nose* during minute 3 on the recording sheet.)
Mother: (Shows David a doll and points to its nose.) "Say nose."
David: "Nose."
Mother: "Good, David." (She smiles, gives David a chocolate chip, and father records his response—*nose*.)

Mother then went on to teach *eye* and *mouth* in the same way. She finished the session by rehearsing both the new words David learned and the names of body parts that he knew previously.

Before beginning the teaching session, David's mother made several preparations to insure that the session would go well. She started by picking a good *place* for working on talking. She chose a quiet room where she and David would not be disturbed. The television and radio were turned off, and there were no toys around to distract David from listening to his mother's instructions. She sat opposite David so that he could see her lips clearly when she spoke because it helped David to imitate the words she asked him to say.

David's mother chose a *time* of day when she would not be distracted and when David was alert and ready to concentrate on the speech lesson. She decided to conduct the session 1 hour before bedtime. This was a time when David was still alert, looked forward to her company, and was ready for a snack. In addition, David's father was home and able to observe and record the session. In short, this is a convenient time for David's family. The morning might be more convenient for another family. If there are no siblings or older siblings that go off to school and if a friend is willing to record your child's speech, midmorning might be the best time for you and your child.

David's mother also made sure that she planned the session well before beginning. She prepared a *word list* that included both the words David knew well and the new words she planned to teach that day. She looked at the list whenever she needed to know what words to rehearse or introduce during the session. Using the list helped David's mother keep the session running at a smooth and steady pace. She did not have to stop to figure out what to do next, and David did not have a chance to get bored or distracted while waiting.

David's mother *organized* the session to help him feel successful and to encourage him to work hard. The session began and finished on a positive note. She spent the first 2 minutes rehearsing words that David knew well so that he would be successful at the start of the session. The rehearsal of familiar words put him in a good mood for the harder work to come. David's mother switched to teaching new words during the next 8 minutes, a time when the growth occurs. Before ending the session, she again spent 2 minutes rehearsing familiar words. By using this strategy, David's mother made sure that he started and ended the session performing successfully. This initial and concluding success helped to keep David in a good mood, motivated him to work hard, and allowed him to gain a sense of achievement in his efforts at talking. Because she began and finished with easy requests, not only was David successful, but he enjoyed the session.

The final preparations made by David's mother before beginning the teaching session were to get some chocolate chips to use as food rewards, a pencil to record David's speech, and a doll to use as a prop in teaching. *Rewards* and *speech records* are important parts of the language training program, and they are discussed in detail in other chapters of this manual. David's mother used the doll as a prop to make the session more interesting and to help David understand the meanings of the words she was teaching. She kept the props close at hand, but out of David's sight until they were needed. She learned that David pays attention best when she uses only one prop at a time, so when she has more than one, she hides the others from his view. If there are too many props around, David may become distracted and pay attention to them rather than to what his mother is saying.

It may be helpful to summarize the points presented thus far about the language teaching sessions. To insure the success of the teaching sessions, it is important to carry out the following preparations:

1. Choose a *place* for teaching that is quiet, comfortable, and free from distractions. Sit opposite your child so that he or she can see your face clearly when you speak.
2. Choose a *time* of day when you and your child are alert and able to concentrate on talking.
3. Use a *word list* to help remember the words your child knows well and the words you plan to teach.
4. *Organize* the session so that your child starts and ends performing successfully.
5. Have the food *rewards* and props you plan to use close at hand.
6. *Record* the speech your child produces during the 12-minute session.

Rewards are an important part of your child's everyday life. They come in many different forms—praise, hugs, kisses, ice cream, trips to the playground—and they all bring pleasure to your child. In fact, anything that increases the probability of a response is a reward. Anything that your child likes or wants will serve as a reward and increase the probability of a response—in this case, talking. Rewards are especially important in the productive language teaching session because they motivate children to pay attention and to work at learning to talk.

The use of contingent consequences (giving a reward for a desired behavior)—including social responses, desired objects, and edibles as rewards for talking—communicates to children that they have done something important and valuable and serves to encourage a child's use of productive language. Social rewards are extremely important, particularly when provided by a child's parent. They include such things as a smile, a pat on the head, a hug, saying "Good girl" or "Good boy," clapping, or just looking at your child approvingly. Praise and attention in many forms serve as social rewards.

Providing an object that your child wants when he or she says a word is a form of reward that is most like the naturally occurring consequences for talking. When a little boy looks up at a shelf and says car and his father retrieves it for him, he receives a reward for talking that is directly related to his reason for using the word. The vocal utterance car conveyed a thought or wish that this child had and changed that thought into a fulfilled wish. This kind of consequence for talking normally occurs frequently when children are learning to talk. Desired consequences should be produced as often as possible because it is the form of reward that is consistent with the use of productive language for communication. Whenever possible during the language sessions, require your child to name an object before receiving it. Thus, a mother may take a ball from a bag and ask, "What's this?" If the child says ball, she should receive the ball to play with momentarily; if she does not say ball or an approximation, she should not receive the object. The same use of contingencies should be required during the course of the day. For example, outside the sessions, she should be required to say open before a door is opened, juice before given her snack, and up before she is lifted and carried.

Food rewards are used in combination with social rewards and desired objects because they provide additional incentives and strengthen and accelerate learning. Unlike social rewards that occur during the day in other situations, distinctive food rewards such as chocolate chips or raisins can be limited to the teaching session and, as such, can retain their reward value. There are times when praise alone is not effective. Food rewards are particularly helpful when you are trying to teach your child new material during the middle working phase of the session, but they are also helpful to start and finish the session on a pleasurable note. In other words, the contingent use of social and food rewards together with a desired object provides greater leverage and increases your effectiveness as a teacher.

Food rewards are used in this program because they promote quicker success. They strongly motivate children to speak and make it easier for them to understand what they are asked to do during the language sessions. When a child is given a chocolate chip immediately after saying a word, it helps the child understand that speaking is the appropriate activity. Moreover, there are many instances in which a desired object cannot be given contingently. For example, one function of language involves simple naming. Running, moon, dog, and crying do not demand a response, but food rewards will help to highlight and strengthen the child's use of these words. The use of praise, the desired object, and food rewards "contingent upon" or following a child's speech, is itself a form of behavioral communication that the child understands. The rewards say loudly and clearly, "That was good." By giving the rewards only when talking occurs, your child will receive a clear behavioral message that is easy to understand: "If you want a food reward, you must speak." Although children normally learn to speak without the systematic use of food rewards, children with delayed talking appear to learn faster and easier if food rewards are used.

The use of food rewards is discussed frequently throughout this language teaching program. However, it should be emphasized that the use of food is a temporary practice and that desired objects and praise are equally important. Food rewards are used to facilitate the learning of new words and phrases, but they are used less frequently as children become more competent talkers. The use of food rewards helps parents to respond to talking contingently, and children soon learn to talk readily. Food rewards help the parent to learn a new style of interaction because the response is easy to define, observable, and easily documented. Thus, the use of food rewards is as important for parents as it is for children, but both needs will diminish as your child begins to speak competently.

We want to dismiss one possible concern immediately: Children *do not* become dependent on food rewards to continue talking as a result of this program. There are at least three reasons for this. First, food rewards are systematically diminished toward the end of this program using a procedure called "partial reward" in which food rewards are given only some of the time rather than for every spoken word. Second, praise and attention should *always* be given along with food to reward speech. As your child becomes a more competent speaker, the use of food rewards may be decreased, and social rewards alone will become sufficient to motivate your child to talk. Third, talking brings its own naturally occurring rewards, which may take many forms. For example, picking up a child who says *up* is a rewarding experience in its own right; that is to say, completion of the act is its own reward that strengthens talking naturally. Eventually, talking for its own sake will become far more important than talking simply for food.

CHOOSING REWARDS

Rewards are an essential part of the language teaching sessions. Anything that will increase the probability of a particular response can serve as a reward. Thus, rewards can come in many forms. Three kinds of rewards—praise, a desired object, and edibles—have uses in this program, which need to be explained.

On a practical level, there are at least two important considerations in choosing and giving rewards. First, the rewards you choose should be "rewarding" to your child. They should be types of praise and attention that your child particularly enjoys and foods that he or she likes to eat. Social rewards that most children enjoy include clapping, smiling brightly, saying "Good girl" or "Good boy," and hugging or patting. Toys or objects that can be given contingently during the training sessions should be interesting and meaningful to the child; preferably, they can be named by one- or two-syllable words. Objects such as a toy car, truck, bus, boat, ball, baby, doll, dog, cat, and hat are appropriate because they are meaningful to young children and relatively easy to say. Successful food rewards are often distinctive in taste such as mini-chocolate chips, bits of mint chocolate, M & M's (or pieces of them), small pieces of potato chips or cheese crackers, some dry cereals, jello, raisins, ice cream, bits of fruit, or juice. Second, food rewards should be available in very small pieces that are easy to chew and swallow. The pleasure of the reward should be short so that your child is soon ready to work for another taste. Chewy candies like taffy or large pieces of cookie are poor rewards because they take too long to eat, satisfy a child's hunger too quickly, and often do not have a distinctive taste.

Before reading further, it might be helpful to stop and make a list of the different object, social, and food rewards that you think will work well with your child. Write them down in the manual and refer to the list when you are planning rewards to use during the teaching sessions.

SOCIAL REWARDS   *OBJECT REWARDS*   *FOOD REWARDS*

1. _____   1. _____   1. _____

2. _____   2. _____   2. _____

3. _____   3. _____   3. _____

It is a good idea to set aside two or three food rewards so that you can vary them if necessary. Your child's preferences may change from day to day, and having different rewards available will help you respond to these changes. In order for your child to work for a reward, he or she must want that particular treat. In other words, a desire for the food reward must be present for it to function as an incentive. Similarly, a child must desire attention from his or her parents and be interested in and want the objects that are presented as rewards if they are to be effective. If a child shows no interest in a particular object, it is not likely to be an effective reward and should be strengthened by combining it with praise and/or a desired edible. One problem with social rewards is that although they are power-ful, they sometimes lose their effectiveness during the relatively long and concentrated interactions that occur during the 12-minute teaching ses-sions.

Food rewards are used in addition to praise and desired objects because they have at least four strengths. First, edibles as rewards bring a clear and objective precision to the task. Some parents report that it is easier to understand and learn a contingent style of interaction using food rewards because the procedure is always the same from one time to the next. Second, tiny edibles are simple to prepare and administer during the sessions. Many objects that represent appropriate first words for teach-ing, such as *ball, hat,* and *car,* either lose their attractiveness, are hard to find, or become boring quickly and, therefore, lose their usefulness. On the other hand, food rewards generally maintain their effectiveness be-cause children, like adults, can be counted on to be hungry at certain times of the day. As a result, less time is often needed to prepare effective food rewards than equally effective object rewards for the sessions. Third, both the incentive and reward values of edibles tend to remain high for long periods. That is to say, food rewards can be counted on to remain more desirable to your child both within a given session and over different sessions occurring over days and even weeks. As a result, edibles are often more stable rewards than praise or objects and represent a highly effective lever for generating productive language. The importance of delayed speech as a developmental problem and the effectiveness of ed-ibles in producing a solution justifies their use. Fourth, the presentation of edibles contingent upon correct talking is a simple procedure that most parents can understand and master easily. In other words, the use of edibles during the teaching sessions is a precise way for parents to learn how to interact contingently with their children.

GIVING REWARDS

Once a particular food reward has been selected, it should be given to your child during the teaching sessions only. For example, if chocolate chips are the chosen reward, do not give them to your child at other times during the day; save chocolate as a reward for the teaching sessions only. If a child is given food rewards for no special reason at other times of the day, the food reward will cease to be a treat, its desirability will diminish, and your child may not be motivated to work for the food during the teaching session. In addition, the behavioral message contained in the contingent use of rewards that tells the child nonverbally that he or she did something special will be blurred if that food reward is used in other circumstances. Restricting the reward to the teaching session is a clear message to your child that chocolate, for example, is earned only when he or she speaks. In addition, children should be encouraged to eat the food reward immediately after it is given. Saving rewards should be discouraged because it may create a distraction and diminish the child's desire to speak. It is better to reduce the number of food rewards if they are beginning to accumulate.

It is important to remember that food rewards work best when a child is a little bit hungry. Teaching sessions held immediately after a meal may not work unless you plan to use part of the meal, like dessert, for a reward. Sessions held right before meals also might not work well because a child may be too hungry to think about anything but food. Withholding a food reward when an incorrect response occurs—an essential practice for the effective use of rewards—may prove too frustrating and disruptive when a child is too hungry. Therefore, parents should try to schedule the productive language sessions between meals so that your child will be motivated sufficiently by the food reward, but still able to concentrate on talking.

What Is an Effective Way to Use Rewards?

Consider an example of how one mother responded to her child's attempt to speak. Leslie and her mother were sitting opposite each other on the floor in the living room. Mother was teaching Leslie to say the word *ball*.

Mother:	(Holds up a ball and points to it.) "Leslie, say ball."
Leslie:	"Mm."
Mother:	(Does not reward Leslie.) "Ball. Ball. Leslie, say ball."
Leslie:	"Buh."
Mother:	(Rewards Leslie by placing a raisin in her mouth as she praises her.) "Good girl. You said ball."
Leslie:	"Buh."
Mother:	(Rewards Leslie by giving her another raisin as she praises her.) "Good girl. You said ball. Leslie, say ball."
Leslie:	"Ball."
Mother:	(Rewards Leslie again. This time, mother gives Leslie a hug as she praises her, gives her a raisin, and lets her throw the ball.) "Yeah Leslie! You said ball!"

One of the most important things to learn about using rewards is that they are given to your child *only* when he or she responds correctly to a request with a word or word approximation. Receiving rewards must be contingent upon a correct performance if rewards are to increase your child's productive language. Therefore, it is important to know what you want your child to say and what you will accept as a correct response so that you can use rewards appropriately. In our example, Leslie's mother did not reward her for saying *Mm* because the word she asked Leslie to say was *ball,* and the *Mm* sound was too different. Not receiving a reward was a clear nonpunitive message to Leslie that her response was incorrect and that she would have to try again.

How to Determine When a Response Is Correct

What you consider a correct response should depend on how well your child can say the word that he or she is asked to repeat. When first learning a new word, your child should be rewarded even if the response is only partially correct. In our example, Leslie was rewarded for saying *buh* when her mother asked her to say *ball.* Leslie's response was "almost correct," and rewarding it let her know that she was on the right track, that *buh* was close enough for now. After a few attempts, Leslie succeeded in saying the whole word *ball,* and her mother rewarded her enthusiastically with praise, a raisin, and the ball itself.

Almost correct responses should not be rewarded after your child has produced a completely correct response three or four times. In our example, Leslie's mother should not reward her for saying only *buh* after Leslie says *ball* a few times. It is important to reward your child's best responses *each* time they occur, particularly when your child is learning to produce a new word. "Consistent" or "continuous" rewards for each correct response are essential when new learning is occurring. Consistent rewards will let children know when their responses are correct and will encourage them to keep trying. Consistent rewards for *each* best response are the most effective way to help your child learn any new material.

The shift from an almost correct response *(buh)* to a correct response *(ball)* may require several teaching sessions, so you should avoid "getting stuck" on one word. If after five or six successful approximations of *buh* your child has not produced the correct sound *ball,* simply move on to another word. *It is far more important that your child acquire many almost correct responses than pronounce one or two words perfectly at this stage of the process.* Put another way, it is more desirable that your child experience the success of producing many almost correct responses than risk the boredom and resistance that may result from demanding perfect articulation for a few words. This choice is particularly important in the beginning of the program when progress may be slow and the learning of new spoken words fragile.

The Role of Partial Reward

Paradoxically, once a word is well learned and your child can say it easily, he or she should not be rewarded with food for every correct response. This is a surprising, counterintuitive fact that bears repeating. After a word is well learned, it is sufficient to give a food reward only every second or third time that your child says the word. One way to do this is to provide attention and praise alone each time the word is spoken, but to use food rewards more sparingly at this point. This procedure, called *partial reward*, helps strengthen your child's existing vocabulary and encourages him or her to work harder. Rather than one response, your child will learn to make several correct responses before receiving a food reward. As a result, your child will talk more, get more practice, and be less likely to forget what has already been learned.

Partial reward also makes your job as a teacher easier because you no longer have to give food rewards for every correct response. Once your child gains a new word and repeats it on request readily, you can switch to using food rewards only some of the time. Praise and attention will be sufficient to maintain your child's use of that word, freeing time and energy for you to concentrate on other new words. Even though food may be given less frequently, you should continue to praise your child often for using a word, particuarly in the beginning.

The Natural Reward Value of Speech

Reducing the frequency of food rewards while continuing the use of attention and praise will help your child learn that words can be used to express his or her thoughts and needs. The ability to communicate verbally brings its own rewards. Eventually, talking itself will be sufficient to motivate your child to learn new words on his or her own, just as children usually do. From your child's perspective, talking is almost a magical event. The ability to talk opens a new and socially desirable way for your child to control his or her world. A child can sound a word and receive a drink of juice, form another word and get picked up, utter still another sound and have a favorite toy retrieved. When children can communicate easily with others, they can ask for attention, make their needs known to those who can help, and gain their own rewards. Thus, effective verbal communication brings its own rewards, maintains itself, and is rarely lost once it is soundly acquired.

We have focused mainly on social and food rewards in our discussion of the teaching sessions, but these are not the only kinds of rewards that can be used. The contingent presentation of desired objects is also useful.

Toys and small objects can be given immediately after they have been named during the training sessions. The objects can provide additional incentives for your child to talk.

Almost anything that satisfies a child's desires and needs can function as a reward, as the discussion about verbal communication implies. Picking up a child can function as a reward for saying *up,* or opening a door when a child says *door* can be a reward. One mother even reported bouncing a ball off the top of her head as a way of rewarding her child for saying *ball.* Playing a favorite game, going to the park, having father read a favorite story, or playing with friends can also be used to reward a particularly good session. Each of these desired activities represents an especially good way to supplement the smaller rewards of praise, objects, and food used during the teaching session. Obviously, many different things can function as rewards, and if presented contingently, they can serve to stimulate and strengthen talking.

It is a good practice to follow up particularly successful productive language sessions with one of the larger rewards. Occasionally, provide ice cream or a trip to the playground as a special treat when a good session occurs, but let your child know why you are doing it. Finally, remember that talking will eventually become its own reward, no matter how difficult talking may be for your child.

BRIEF REVIEW

Before ending our discussion of rewards, three points should be emphasized. First, social, object, and food rewards are most effective when given *immediately* after a correct response. Quick delivery helps your child identify what he or she did to earn the reward and encourages learning. Second, it is also helpful to tell your child exactly why he or she is receiving the reward as you give it. In our example at the beginning of this chapter, Leslie's mother said, "You said ball" to explain to Leslie why she was praised and given a raisin. The explanation made it easier for Leslie to learn that *ball* was the correct response. Third, social rewards should be given with enthusiasm. It is important to be animated and lively, to let your child know clearly that you are pleased with his or her speech. A raisin accompanied by an enthusiastic and animated "Good for you!" is more likely to please your child and instill a feeling of success than giving the raisin alone. Be enthusiastic when your child is successful, even if you are tired and do not feel like a cheerleader at the moment. Energetically given praise is more likely to be effective than a ho-hum response.

Choosing Rewards

1. Choose types of praise and attention that your child particularly enjoys and favorite objects and foods that he or she prefers as rewards.
2. Food rewards should be available in very small pieces that are easy to chew and swallow.
3. Food rewards should be reserved for the teaching sessions and not generally available or given indiscriminately.

Giving Rewards

1. Rewards work best when given immediately after a correct response.
2. Reward *newly learned* words with praise and food each time they are said.
3. Reward *well-learned* words with praise and attention at all times, but use food rewards only every second or third time the words are said.
4. Give rewards enthusiastically. Be animated and lively with your praise and attention.

HOW TO MEASURE YOUR CHILD'S SUCCESS

Recording Productive Language

It should be stated immediately that recording occasional sessions is desirable. However, if you dislike record keeping so much that it may interfere with your willingness to conduct the sessions on a regular basis, then forget the records. Some families may find recording extremely difficult to arrange. In these cases, it may be better to skip the records than to allow them to dampen your enthusiasm for the training sessions themselves. If you can record the sessions about once or twice each week, then do it. The records can and will be extremely helpful to you.

The words spoken by your child during each teaching session should be recorded so that his or her progress with the productive language program can be measured. This information is useful for evaluating the success of your efforts and for planning the words to be taught in subsequent sessions. Recording the productive language sessions will let you know which words your child knows well and which words need practice. In addition, the records let you evaluate how much language your child has learned and which teaching techniques are most helpful.

The easiest way to record your child's efforts at talking is to have two adults, often mother and father, participate in the teaching session. One person should act as the teacher, prompting and rewarding speech, and the other should record all of the words or sounds produced during the 12-minute session. During the teaching session, the recorder should sit out of your child's sight and remain quiet in order to minimize distractions and disruptions.

The recording of speech requires a watch with a second hand and a one-page recording sheet like the one illustrated in Fig. 4.1. A separate recording sheet should be filled out for each 12-minute teaching session. Copies can be xeroxed from this page. There is space at the top of each recording sheet to write in the following information: your child's name, the date, and the names of the people serving as the teacher and the recorder. This information, particularly the date, will be important to you when you look back at your child's progress. The center of the recording sheet is divided into 12 blocks, one for each minute of the teaching session. The recorder should list in the first block all the words produced by your child during the first minute of the session. Speech produced during the second minute should be recorded in the second block and so on until the 12 blocks are completed and the teaching session is finished.

There are two important procedures to follow when recording productive language. First, try to record your child's sounds and words exactly as they are spoken. For example, if he or she says *noh* for *nose* or *buh* for *ball*, write *noh* and *buh* on the recording sheet. This will let you measure your child's progress in fine detail. Second, if your child says a word more than once, write it out the first time it occurs and record repetitions with slash marks following the word. For example, if your child says *hat* three times and *milk* two times, you should write:

hat//
milk/

It is helpful if the recorder writes down the words that you asked your child to say, whether he or she says them or not. If an entire minute goes by without a word from your child, you should still know the words that were requested. At the end of the session, go back and think about why your child refused to say certain words. Were they too long or too difficult to say? Did you ask your child to say multiple-syllable abstract words rather than one-syllable concrete nouns, for example? Did you allow your child enough time to answer? It is important to be patient and allow time for your child to try to answer your question, but a common error for adults is to talk too quickly. Was there a distraction? Should the recorder find a different seat, for example? Was your child resistant and un-cooperative? If your child was crying or turning away, it may be neces-

NAME _____	DATE _____	TEACHER	CODER

Record each word to occur during each minute block for all 12 minutes.

Minute 1	2	3	4
5	6	7	8

9	10	11	12

Number of:

Sounds _____   Two-word sequences _____   All words (or sounds) _____

Single words _____   Three+ word sequences _____   Different words (or sounds) _____

FIG. 4.1.   Recording sheet to be xeroxed for language sessions. Copyright Zelazo, P. R., Kearsley, R. B., and Ungerer, J. *Learning to Speak: An Manual for Parents.* Hillsdale, NJ: Lawrence Erlbaum Associates, 1984.

sary to shape compliance to motor activities during separate sessions, for example. The answers to these questions can be used to isolate problems and make the next teaching session more successful.

Scoring the Sessions

A simple count of the total number of words spoken during a 12-minute session is one of the most important measures you will use. Two measures—the total number of words and the total number of *different* words—will capture most of the changes that you will be looking for. Spaces for these totals are given at the bottom of the recording form. Fill in this information at the end of each teaching session. These measures indicate the type and number of words and sounds produced during the 12-minute session. The total number of measures that we have used is eight. The first four depend on your child's level of productive language development and whether your child is using sounds, single words, or two- or three-plus word sentences. These four measures are useful if you are interested in your child's progress over a longer range of time, say, 2 to 4 months. The second four measures—the total number of all words (or all sounds) and the total number of different words (or different sounds)— will provide the most useful information and reflect changes that occur over a shorter period of time, say, 2 to 4 weeks. Thus, these four measures will probably be the most sensitive ones for you to watch and will reflect changes in your child's progress most quickly.

One point should be emphasized: It is necessary to record sounds *only* if your child has few words–say six or less. In this case, the total number of sounds and the number of different sounds will be important indicators of progress. The different sounds, in particular, will be important for selecting appropriate word approximations to encourage. A sound such as *buh* can be matched to the word *ball* and *i* to *eye,* for example.

The eight measures that we have used can be briefly described as follows:

1. *Positive sounds,* for example, distinctive positive vocalizations including vowels, and consonants such as ah, ēē, wuh, and mm.
2. *Single words,* for example, cup, book, cookie.
3. *Two-word sequences,* for example, my cup, big ball, fall down, want juice.
4. *Three-plus words sequences,* for example, I want juice, Mommy give cookie.
5. *Total number of words produced* in the session. Each spoken word should be counted separately even if there are many repetitions of

the same word. Count a two-word sequence as two words and a three-word sequence as three words. The total number of words spoken during a session is a good indication of your child's tendency to talk and is the most sensitive measure in the beginning.

6. *Total number of sounds* produced in the session. Each sound or positive vocalization should be counted separately even if there are many repetitions of the same sound. The total number of positive (non cry) sounds produced during a session is a good indication of your child's tendency to *attempt* talking. Vocalizations are a prerequisite for talking. Increases in the total number of sounds appears to lead to spontaneous increases in the total number of different sounds.

7. *Total number of different words* produced in the session. Repetitions are not counted in this category, only different words. The number of different words spoken is a good estimate of your child's growing vocabulary. In addition, it is an important measure to indicate when your child is ready to use two-word sentences. As a thumbnail guide, when your child has approximately 60 different words, including nouns, verbs, possessives, and other parts of speech, he or she is probably ready to generate two-word sentences.

8. *Total number of different sounds* produced in the session. Repetitions are not counted in this category, only different sounds. The number of different sounds sets the stage for appropriate new word approximations to encourage. Sounds such as *nuh* can be matched to simple, one syllable nouns such as *nose.*

A sample recording sheet with words spoken during a 12-minute session is shown in Fig. 4.2. Many points that we have already discussed can be gleaned from this sample sheet. It can be seen that although this child used only 12 different words, they were spoken 49 times (total words) during the 12-minute session. Moreover, it can be seen that no two-word phrases were produced. It is clear that there were many repetitions, indicating a great deal of practice with a relatively small number of words. The first and last 2 minutes contained relatively simple language in contrast to the middle 8 minutes. Imitation of relatively simple well learned words during the first and last 2 minutes insured a successful beginning and finish. Four new words—car, ball, dog, and pants were introduced during the middle part of the session. This child's mother realized that the word *pants* was too difficult and correctly dropped it. Note also that fewer words were spoken during the middle part of the session because new (and hence, harder) words were introduced. This is expected. An excellent strategy that this mother used was to ask, "What's this?" or "Who's

NAME _____   DATE __6/12__   CODER _____

(im) = imitation;   (Wt) = What's this?

Record each word to occur during each minute block for all 12 minutes.

	TEACHER	Mother	Father

Minute 1
(im) mama (mama)
(im) dada (daddy)
(im) cup (cup)
(Wt) cup
(im) up
(im) dahn (down)

2
(im) nose (nose)
(Wt) nose
(Wt) eye
(Wt) mouth
(Wt) ear
(Wt) ear
(Wt) nose

3
(im) dada (daddy)
(Wt) nose
(Wt) eye
(Wt) ear
(Wt) mouth
(im) dahn (down)

4
(im) eh (pants)
(im) eh (pants)
(im) (pants)
(im) ca (car)
(im) cah (car)
(Wt) ca (car)

5
(Wt) cah
(im) ba (ball)
(im) ball (ball)
(im) ball (ball)

6
(Wt) ball
(Wt)
(im) ca (car)
(im) cah (car)
(car)

7
(Wt) cah
(Wt)
(im) uh (dog)
(im) da (dog)

8
(im) da (dog)
(im) doh (dog)
(Wt) doh
(Wt) doh

9
(Wt) cah
(Wt) ball
(Wt)
(im) doh (dog)
(Wt)

10
(Wt) doh
(Wt) doh
(Wt) cah
(Wt) ball
(Wt) cup

11
(Wt) nose
(Wt) eye
(Wt) ear
(Wt) mouth
(Wt) nose

12
(Wt) mama
(im) up (up)
(im) down (down)
(Wt) mama
(Wt) nose
(Wt) mouth
(Wt) eye

Number of: Sounds _9_   Two-word sequences _0_   All words (or sounds) _49_

Single words _49_   Three⁺ word sequences _0_   Different words (or sounds) _12_

FIG. 4.2. Recording sheet with words spoken during a 12-minute session.

70

this?" immediately after the child imitated the new word. This procedure should be attempted whenever possible because it encourages retrieval from memory, not just simple matching of a spoken to a heard sound.

An Option: Illustrating the Results

The word totals for each day's session can also be graphed to produce a clear visual record of each week's progress, but this is not essential. If the task of graphing the results is too burdensome to you, feel free to skip this section and go to the next section on alternative recording strategies. If you are not interested in graphing the daily and weekly outcomes, you might simply examine the totals for each day over the course of a week or month. The purpose of this section is to show you how to illustrate the total number of words and of different words for each session. By graphing the totals for each day, you will be able to determine whether talking increased over the days and weeks that you have conducted the training sessions.

For those of you who wish to create a visual picture of your child's progress over the course of a week, we have included an example of a typical week's productive language output in Fig. 4.3. A sample summary page for creating a graph is shown in Fig. 4.4. The total number of occurrences for any of the measures for any one day can be listed on the face sheet shown in the figure. This summary sheet contains spaces for seven sessions along the horizontal (bottom) axis—typically 1 full week of training. There are spaces along the bottom line for listing each day. The vertical line is left blank deliberately so that it can be adjusted for each child according to his or her particular level of word production.

The numbers to choose for the vertical line can be determined by writing the total number of words for the first session in the third heavy horizontal line that intersects with the vertical (up and down) axis. Let each *heavy* horizontal mark along this vertical axis represent 10 points. For example, suppose that a child produced a total of 30 words during the first session. It would be appropriate to allow each heavy line along the vertical axis to equal 10 words, producing 0 at the bottom and 60 at the top. This choice is arbitrary and may change from week to week depending on your child's progress. The objective is simply to create a visual impression of your child's performance. By allowing space above and below your child's first day total, there will be room to reflect changes upward or downward over the remaining 6 days. If progress is steadily upward, it may be best to place the first day's total, 30 in this case, on the second horizontal line.

Consider an example. To plot the first day's total, list the date on the first space along the bottom line, count up to three heavy bars, and place a

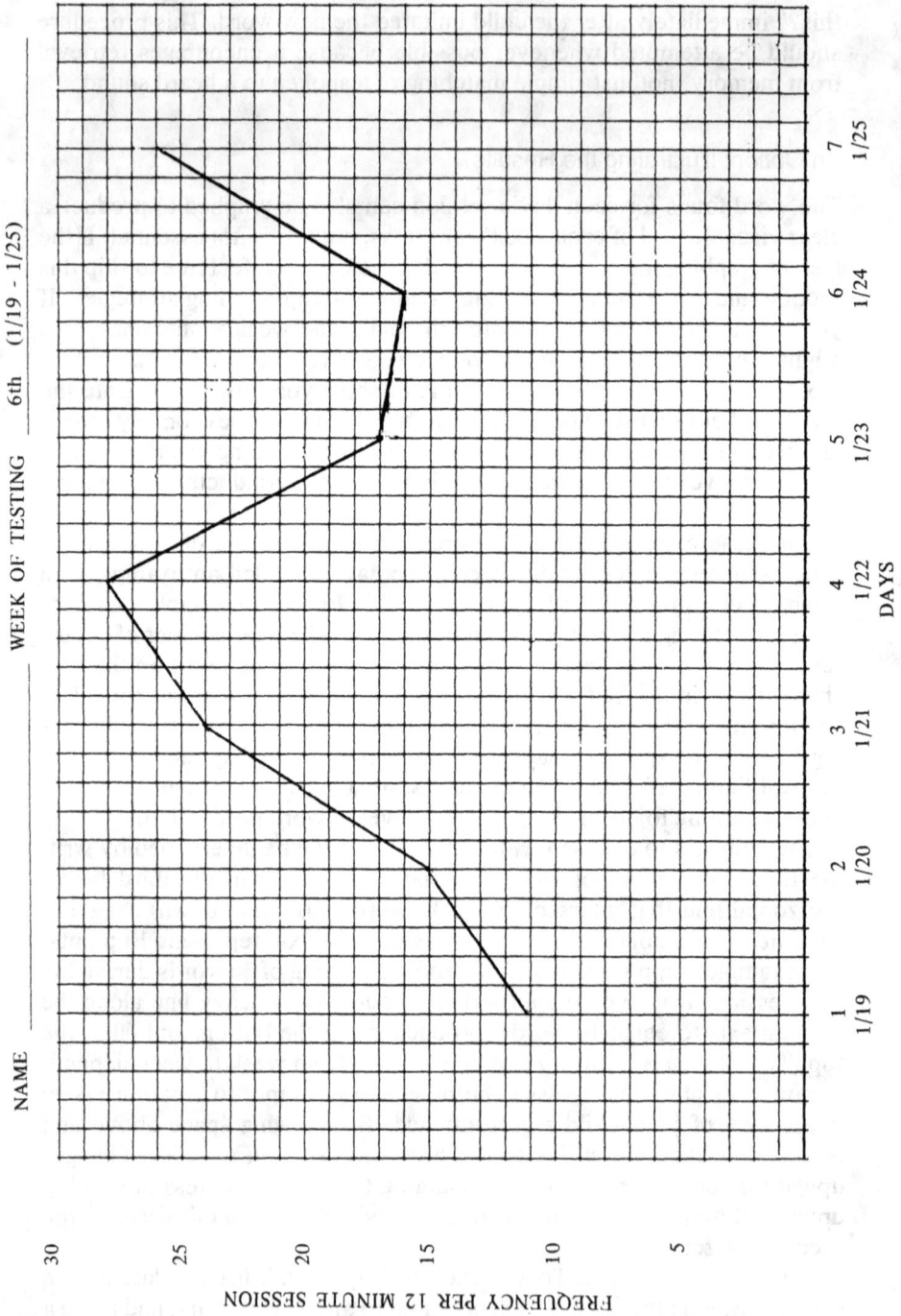

NAME _____   WEEK OF TESTING ___ 6th ___ (1/19 - 1/25)

FREQUENCY PER 12 MINUTE SESSION

30

25

20

15

10

5

1   2   3   4   5   6   7
1/19   1/20   1/21   1/22   1/23   1/24   1/25

DAYS

(List dates of testing)

72

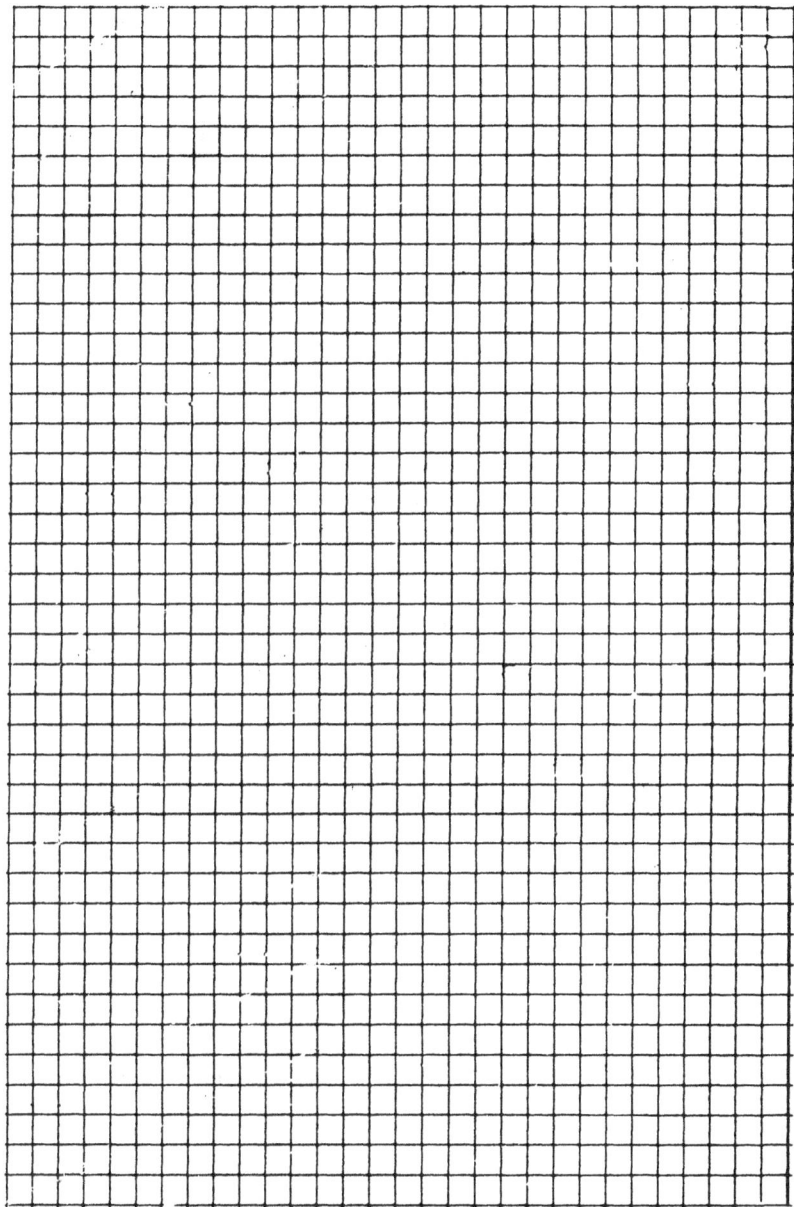

FIG. 4.4. Summary sheet to be xeroxed to illustrate words spoken each day for one week. Copyright Zelazo, P. R., Kearsley, R. B., and Ungerer, J. *Learning to Speak: A Manual for Parents.* Hillsdale, NJ: Lawrence Erlbaum Associates, 1984.

DAYS

(List dates of testing)

FREQUENCY PER 12 MINUTE SESSION

73

dot where the vertical and horizontal lines cross. Move over to the next heavy vertical line. Insert the correct date. Move up the vertical line to the horizontal line corresponding to the score that you wish to plot for this day. Repeat this process for each day. Connect the points to form a pattern depicting your child's progress over the 7 days of training.

The main reason for keeping a graph is to provide a visual image of your child's progress over any seven sessions of training. *Do not allow this task to become complex or tedious; if it does, skip it.* It should also be mentioned that the curve or graph produced by connecting the points for each day is likely to have increases and decreases. However, in general, the curve should have an upward pattern as shown in Fig. 4.3.

Alternative Recording Strategies

If another person is not available to record the teaching sessions, one of two alternative strategies can be used: (1) a tape recorder can be used to record productive language for 12 minutes; (2) a checklist can be prepared in advance and checked off during the sessions. *It is too confusing to be both teacher and recorder; we do not recommend it.* If a tape recorder is used, be sure to announce the beginning and end of the session on the tape so that you can score the results for each minute if you wish. Play the tape back at the end of the session and use a watch with a second hand to determine the appropriate 1-minute blocks on the sheet used to record your child's speech (see Fig. 4.1). Complete the tabulations at the bottom of the sheet and graph the results if you like. An added benefit to this technique is that the tape that you make can be used as a reward for your child at the end of the session. Many parents report that their children enjoy hearing the tape recordings of their own speech and talk to the recordings.

If you do not have a tape recorder, you may prefer another option. You can prepare a list of words in advance and check them off as your child produces them. It is easier to check off words than it is to write them down during the session, but this approach, unlike the use of a second person or a tape recorder, has two disadvantages. First, you may lose your child's word approximations when using a checklist; it is difficult to anticipate exactly which sound will be produced for each word, particularly new words. Second, it is often distracting to teach and record at the same time, even with the checklist. Clearly, the more important task is to teach; the primary goal is to elicit productive language and reward each spoken word quickly and enthusiastically. If you are presented with the choice of doing the session without recording or not doing the session at all, then by all means conduct the session without recording. Later, you may recall the new words produced and be able to compile an approximate list of your child's expanding vocabulary. However, the recording of sessions at least once each week using one of these strategies is highly desirable.

Recording productive language verbatim during the sessions without the help of another adult is sometimes difficult, and you may choose to use Table 4.1 to create a checklist to record the speech yourself. A word list can be used to plan the session and serve as a checklist as well. Table 4.1 can be used to create a teaching plan involving a list of familiar and new words with space for recording the number of repetitions of each word and any word approximations the child makes. If your child is cooperative during the session, recording speech may not be difficult. But if he or she is at all resistant, it may be impossible both to record speech and keep the session running smoothly. When this happens, it is best to conduct the session without recording productive language. There is no question that it is better to reward than to record.

The Value of Careful Record Keeping

It is important to keep accurate records of your child's performance during the productive language sessions because this information is useful for evaluating his or her progress and for planning future sessions. The total number of words that your child says in a 12 minute session should increase as your child becomes a more competent speaker. This measure reflects the degree to which your child is able and/or willing to talk. The total number of *different* words that your child uses in a session should also increase as his or her speech improves. This measure reflects an expanding vocabulary and will confirm your child's growing knowledge of the world. The total number of *different* words produced can be counted at the end of each session.

Both the total number of words and the number of different words produced in a 12-minute session are sensitive indicators of your child's progress. Small changes in performance frequently pass unnoticed when records are not kept, yet they are often significant and may announce important gains. For example, a change from using one-word to two-word phrases or even an increase of one or two *new* words during a session may reflect important milestones in your child's progress toward learning to talk. Because the sessions are carefully timed and constant from one day to another, it is likely that even small increases in performance are "real" indications of progress. The timed sessions and controlled conditions make it likely that the changes you see are not simply chance occurrences or the result of a longer session than the previous one. In a sense, these recordings are like temperature readings and can reflect significant differences from day to day, which may go unnoticed otherwise.

TABLE 4.1

Child's Name _____   Date _____

Teacher _____

WORD LIST

Familiar Words & Sentences	No. Responses	New Words & Sentences	No. Responses
1			
2			
3			
4			
5			
6			
7			
8			
9			
10			
11			
12			
13			
14			
15			
16			
17			
18			
19			
20			
21			
22			
23			
24			
25			
26			
27			
28			
29			
30			

Total   Single Words   _____   Different   Single Words   _____
        2-Word Sentences   _____   2-Word Sentences _____
        3-Word Sentences   _____   3-Word Sentences _____

An additional advantage derived from obtaining accurate and frequent records is that as parents you and the professionals who may follow your child will be able to see the progress that your child makes from one week to the next. In a way, these records are your reward for the time and effort that you have put into helping your child learn to speak. Teaching is more enjoyable and rewarding when you can see the changes that your efforts are producing. If conditions are not similar from one day to the next, if the lengths of the sessions vary, and if careful records are not kept, it is impossible to determine if small but significant improvement occurs. Without evidence of improvement, the effectiveness of the procedures will be in doubt, and you may terminate the program prematurely. Thus, the recordings allow you to be confident that the sessions are working. Without these careful readings, you may become discouraged, "pull back," or even give up prematurely.

During the early stages of learning to speak, progress is sometimes slow and the changes small. These careful recordings can provide sensitive "instrument" readings that indicate that the sessions are producing significant improvement. When your child is in an uncertain and contradictory period of productive language acquisition and you cannot tell whether there is progress, it may become essential to "trust your instrument readings."

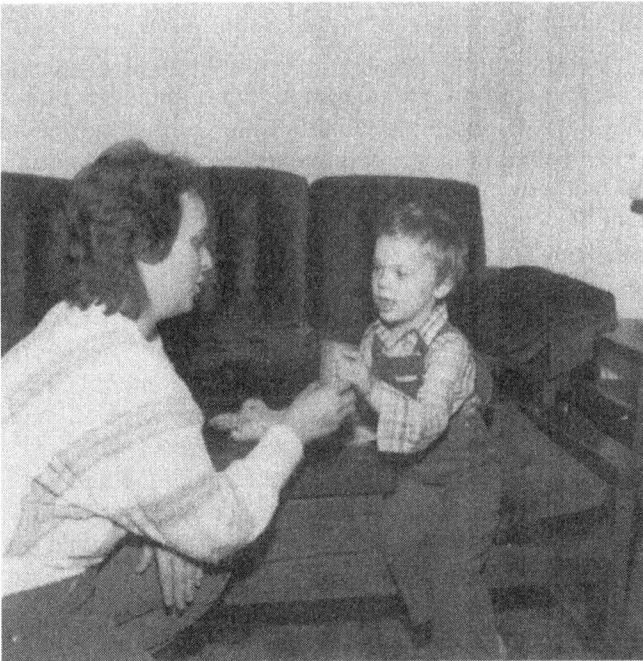

5 Teaching Single Words

INTRODUCTION

The first major goal of the language program is to teach your child to say about 60 different single words. This vocabulary should include words for naming objects and people, greeting people, and asking for things. For example, words like *car, cup, ball, mom, dad, hi, more, please, run,* and *eat* are particularly useful in your child's beginning vocabulary. Your child should be taught to say the words during the teaching sessions and then to use them appropriately at other times during the day. If your child already can say about 60 different single words including two syllable nouns, verbs and adjectives and use them appropriately to name objects or to communicate with people, you should begin this program with the next chapter, entitled "Teaching Two-Word Sentences." However, it is best to read through this chapter first to become generally familiar with the teaching techniques used in the language training program.

We discuss the manner in which language sessions should be conducted and provide suggestions for choosing the appropriate words to teach. It is important to choose words carefully to insure that your child is successful during the teaching sessions and learns words that he or she is likely to use at other times during the day. Different techniques for teaching words are also described, along with ways to encourage your child to talk outside of the teaching sessions. When children generalize or use productive language appropriately outside of the teaching sessions, it is a clear sign that the words they have learned are meaningful and that they are learning to use language to communicate with others.

DETERMINING YOUR CHILD'S CURRENT LEVEL OF PRODUCTIVE LANGUAGE

To measure your child's present productive language skills, record every word that he or she says for 2 full days using the Spontaneous Speech and Receptive Language Record displayed in Table 5.1. In the left-hand column, record only the words that your child says on his or her own; do not record words that are imitations of what someone else has just prompted your child to say. As you record the productive language, note whether your child uses words in ways that make sense to you. For example, when your child says *more,* is he or she asking you to give more of something to eat or play with? When your child says *car,* is he or she telling you about a car, naming a toy car while playing with it, or asking to go for a ride? Can you usually figure out what your child is trying to say when he or she uses words?

After recording spontaneous talking for 2 days, count up the number of different words your child has said. If you have recorded at least four or five different words that your child uses in a sensible, meaningful way, then he or she is ready to begin this phase of the language program. If your child has said less than two or three words or says no words at all, you should consult with a professional before beginning the program to make sure that there are no medical or neurological reasons for the productive-language delay, that your child's hearing is normal and that the program is appropriate for your child.

In addition to words that your child says, Table 5.1 includes a section to indicate words that your child appears to understand but does not say. These are important words to begin using in the teaching sessions because, if your child understands them, they are likely to be easier to say. A list of the sounds that your child makes, as requested in item 9, can be used to choose similar sounding one-syllable words for the sessions. For example, if your child can make the sound *noh,* the word *nose* may be appropriate to teach. Completion of the other items in the table will provide you with a good assessment of your child's current language ability and you will have a record against which you can judge his or her progress over the weeks of training. It is a good practice to complete Table 5.1 at about 8-week intervals to assess your child's progress.

BEGINNING THE LANGUAGE TEACHING SESSION

Before starting your first teaching session, remember the six preparatory steps outlined in Chapter 4. Once these preparations have been made, you are ready to begin teaching.

TABLE 5.1
Spontaneous Speech and Receptive Language Record

CHILD'S NAME _____   DATES _____

CHILD'S DATE OF BIRTH _____   FORM COMPLETED BY _____

Below is a list of words commonly said or understood by young children. Use this list to help record your child's spontaneous speech for a period of 2 full days. Put a check beside each word your child says during the 2 days and write in any words that he or she says that are not on the list. When recording words, be sure to note any immature pronunciations your child may use like *muh* for *milk*. If you know your child can say a word, but may have not heard it during the 2-day recording period, check it off anyway and mark the check with an asterisk like this √* . Also, use this list to mark off words that your child understands but does not yet say.

Total number of words: spoken _____   understood _____

Total number of two-word phrases _____   three-word phrases _____

BODY PARTS

	Says	Understands but does not say
ear		
eye		
hair		
mouth		
neck		
nose		

HOUSEHOLD

	Says	Understands but does not say
bath		
bed		
bowl		
chair		
clock		
cup		
floor		
fork		

"Household" continued next page

FOOD

	Says	Understands but does not say
apple		
banana		
butter		
candy		
cereal		
coke		
cookie		
gum		
ice cream		
juice		
milk		
orange		
peas		
pizza		
water		

HOUSEHOLD (continued)

	Says	Understands but does not say
knife		
light		
pan		
phone		
plate		
pot		
spoon		
table		

TOYS

	Says	Understands but does not say
ball		
boat		
book		
car		
puzzle		
truck		

TABLE 5.1 (cont'd.)

ANIMALS & PEOPLE

	Says	Understands but does not say
boy		
daddy		
duck		
kitty		
me		
mommy		

CLOTHING

	Says	Understands but does not say
blouse		
boot		
dress		
hat		
pants		
shirt		
shoe		
sock		

OTHER

	Says	Understands but does not say
bye bye		
clean		
come		
do		
don't		
eat		
go		
gone		
hi		
hot		
in		
kiss		
more		
my		
off		
on		
out		
please		
see		
sorry		
sun		
up		

2) How does your child demonstrate that he or she *knows* the meaning of words?

(a) points to the object or to the picture of the object when you say the word.

(b) when asked "Is this a _____?" will shake head for a yes or no answer appropriately.

(c) will get the object when the word is said, when appropriate.

(d) other. (describe)

3) Check any of these questions and commands that you believe your child knows the meaning of. Also, write on the line provided any specific words that he or she understands when you say these sentences.

For example:

Point to your nose, cup, toy

_____	Point to your _____
_____	Show me your _____
_____	Where is the _____
_____	Get your _____
_____	Eat your _____
_____	Drink your _____
_____	More? _____
_____	Say _____
_____	Go to _____
_____	Put on your _____
_____	Come here _____
_____	Give a kiss/hug _____
_____	No / Stop it / Don't touch _____
_____	Clap your hands _____
_____	*Others* _____

TABLE 5.1 (cont'd.)

4) List all two-word combinations that your child *says*. Check whether they are said frequently or infrequently.

Combinations   *Frequent*   *Infrequent*

5) List all three-word combinations that your child *says*. Check whether they are said frequently or infrequently.

Combinations   *Frequent*   *Infrequent*

6) List typical sentences that your child says, as the child says it, that is, with the same word order. List only those not covered in items 4 and 5.

7) If your child does not say any words, list the *sounds* your child makes (e.g., vowel sounds like e-e-e-, u-u-u-, or others like m-m-m-, b-a-a--. If you think the sounds have any meaning, write in the meaning.

8) Does your child imitate sounds? For example, if you say a word or sound, does your child repeat it or try to repeat it? Explain what your child does in this situation.

9) If your child is not speaking now, did he or she speak at some other time and then appear to stop? If so, when and what sounds or words did he or she say?

85

The first step children should take in the language teaching sessions is to try to imitate the words you ask them to say. This is not an easy task, and at first your child may not understand what you want him or her to do. One way to help your child imitate is to begin by teaching the imitation of actions involving large movements that are easy for a child to see. In addition, you can physically guide your child through large muscle actions in a way that cannot be done with speech. Actions that are good for teaching imitation include the following:

1. Hand clapping.
2. Waving goodbye.
3. Stretching arms upward.
4. Placing hands on head.
5. Patting both knees.
6. Rubbing the stomach.

The techniques you will need to use are demonstrated in the following example of a typical teaching session.

An Illustrative Teaching Session

Michael is sitting in a chair across from his father and is watching him closely. Father was teaching Michael to imitate hand clapping, a task he chose to work on because he knew that hand clapping was something that Michael could do, but not regularly. Moreover, father knew that it was easier to teach imitation of a known action than to teach imitation of something new.

Father: "Michael, clap hands." (Father claps his hands in front of Michael as he talks to him.)

Michael: (Stares at his father with a blank look on his face.)

Father: (Takes Michael's hands and guides them through the action of clapping.) "Clap hands. Clap hands. Good boy, Michael. You're clapping hands." (Father then drops Michael's hands and again claps his own hands in front of Michael.) "Michael, clap hands."

Michael: (Claps his hands two times.)

Father: "Good boy, Michael. You clapped hands." (Father claps hands and gives Michael a raisin. He repeats his request for clapping hands two times and then goes on to teach imitation of waving goodbye and placing his hands on his head. He ends the session by requesting imitation of hand clapping again.)

When your child has learned to imitate three or four different actions, you can start to teach the imitations of words. In the beginning, focus on teaching the imitation of words that your child already knows how to say. Starting with familiar words will make it easier for your child to learn the new task of imitating speech. The Spontaneous Speech Record in Table 5.1 is a good source of words that most children learn first, and it can be used as the word list in preparation for these teaching sessions.

Familiar Words

In order to help you and your child start the language program success-fully and to build a willingness to talk, the first few teaching sessions should focus simply on increasing the number of times your child says the words he or she already knows. This can be accomplished in two ways. First, ask your child to repeat only the most frequently occurring words that you have listed in the Spontaneous Speech and Receptive Language Record during your first four or five sessions. Second, introduce the words said less frequently, but only during the middle of the sessions, generally, for about 1 week or until your child says them consistently. You should ask your child to repeat the familiar (easy) words during the beginning and end of these sessions and the less familiar (more difficult) words during the middle of the sessions. This strategy is used throughout the program and will keep the sessions both productive and rewarding for your child. Remember that keeping the sessions productive and reward-ing will make them enjoyable for your child and successful for you.

Continue to work on familiar words until your child says them consist-ently and understands clearly how to respond to your requests for speech. Repeating familiar words in the beginning will increase your child's willingness to use his or her existing vocabulary and to respond quickly and correctly to your requests for verbal imitation. Once your child is willing to imitate your verbal requests, you will gain an important lever for encouraging the use of new words. Your child will have begun to learn the rules of your new game.

Before starting a session, plan what you are going to ask your child to say. The Spontaneous Speech and Receptive Language Record is a good source of words that your child knows and should be used as the word list for the first teaching sessions. If you choose the structured format, sit opposite your child so that your face can be seen clearly. Remove all distractions, have the food reward that you plan to use *in hand,* (or pocket) and keep the object that you are naming nearby. When asking your child to say a word, keep your instructions short and simple. For example: "Eric! Say *CAR.*" Do not say: "Eric! Mommy wants you to say the word *car.*"

Speak with a clear and lively voice and make sure that your child is looking at your face. If your child says the word soon after you say it, reward him or her enthusiastically with praise, food, and the object named. If your child does not respond, wait a few seconds and repeat the request. Remember to pause long enough between requests to give your child a chance to reply. Counting to yourself from 1 to 5 is a good way to insure enough time. It is important to be patient, particularly in the beginning. Rehearse a word several times before moving on to other words that your child knows and try to start and end each session with your child performing successfully. Success can be insured either by asking for single words that your child already can say or by having your child imitate a familiar motor task such as clapping hands.

If your child is slow to understand the task of saying words, use an older brother or sister, another adult, or a small doll to model word imitation. Treat the model just as you would treat your child. Ask the model to say a word and reward the model enthusiastically with praise, the object, and food when the word is produced. If another person is not available to act as a model, a doll can be used. Ask the doll to say a word and then "make the doll talk" in response. Using a different voice for the doll often adds interest to the game. Praise the doll for imitating and pretend to reward it by holding a bit of food such as a chocolate chip to its mouth. Modeling, either with another person or with a doll, is an excellent way to help your child understand what to do during the teaching sessions and often adds interest to the task.

The Shaping Procedure

If your child will not imitate you when invited to say a word, there are at least two courses of action available. First, you could reward the imitation of motor actions and build a tendency for imitation that can be generalized to talking, as illustrated earlier. Second, you could "shape" talking by creating the conditions that elicit sounds and words and provide rewards when word approximations or words occur. Events and conditions that stimulate and encourage attempts at talking include presenting familiar and interesting objects, naming these objects frequently, and using indirect questions. Both the structured imitation and the less structured shaping strategies lead to the same end point, although the shaping of spontaneous speech may be a slightly more direct route to the goal of spontaneous communication. The primary objective of this manual is to produce spontaneous talking—the use of solicited or unsolicited nonimitative productive language to communicate your child's thoughts and needs.

It is important to realize that imitation is not the end point of talking, although it is an important means to an end. You do not want to teach your child to say "What's this?" after you say "What's this". However, a tendency to imitate an adult's speech can greatly aid the onset of the child's productive language. The shaping of spontaneous speech and the explicit reward of imitative actions (both gestures and verbal) can proceed together, and they generally do. The purpose of this section on shaping is to emphasize that if a word occurs, even if it is not a direct imitation, it should be rewarded in the beginning.

Your child may not imitate you when asked to say *car*. This may be the result of resistance or because he or she simply does not understand you. In either case, the use of toys or objects that your child can name may help to elicit an appropriate word, particularly if he or she is interested in the toy. If your child says an appropriate word, immediate enthusiastic praise, the object itself, and an edible will increase the chance that that particular word will be used appropriately again. This contingent reward will also increase the likelihood that the word you used will be imitated when you ask for it in the future.

An Illustrative Shaping Session

The shaping procedure differs from the imitation procedure in at least one important way. With shaping, you are free to reward any acceptable response, not just the word or sound that you requested. Any response that moves your child in the desired direction is acceptable. The shaping procedure requires a less exact response from your child, but you gain other advantages. The session may produce more talking by your child if he or she resists your requests for imitation. In addition, the sessions may have a chance to become more positive with more rewards for your child. Equally important, your child will begin to learn the game of give and take during these sessions, ultimately giving you the control to elicit imitation.

In the following example, Tommy's mother uses a ball and a toy car as objects to elicit and shape two words that Tommy would say infrequently.

Mother: "Ball, Tommy. This is a ball." (Pauses 5 seconds.) "Ball."

Tommy: (Reaches for the ball.)

Mother: (Withdraws the ball until Tommy makes an effort to say *ball*. Repeats the word to him again.) "Ball. Say ball."

Tommy: (Resists mother's request to say ball, notices the toy car on the chair, looks at mother, and smiles.) "Car."

Mother: (Puts the ball away quickly, brings out the toy car, and offers it to Tommy.) "Good boy, Tommy. Car. You said car." (She puts a chocolate chip in Tommy's mouth.)

Tommy: (Reaches for the car eagerly.) "Car, car."

Mother: "That's right, Tommy. Car." (Places another chocolate chip in Tommy's mouth. She allows Tommy to push the car for about 8 seconds and then gently removes it. Again she presents the car to Tommy.) "What's this?"

Tommy: "Car."

Mother: (Gives Tommy an enthusiastic kiss and the car.) "Good boy, Tommy. Car. That's a car." (She places another chocolate chip in his mouth.)

Because Tommy's mother enthusiastically and consistently rewarded him each time he said *car,* his production of the word was strengthened. Giving a reward for saying *car* was perfectly acceptable, even though Tommy did not imitate his mother's initial request for the word *ball.* She was able to take full advantage of Tommy's spontaneous and appropriate use of the word *car.* By rewarding the appropriate use of *car,* his mother helped shape a tendency for appropriate speech, a strategy that, in time, will help Tommy overcome his reluctance to say the word *ball.*

In the beginning of speech training sessions, the kind of compromise displayed by Tommy's mother is acceptable because it accomplishes two things. First, Tommy said one of the words appropriately (a compromise on Tommy's part) and provided the opportunity for reward. Second, because he was rewarded, (a compromise on his mother's part) the session turned into a positive teaching experience. Had Tommy's mother missed the opportunity, the session might have become a more difficult one characterized by resistance rather than compliance.

Choosing New Words to Teach

When your child is able to say familiar words each time you ask, he or she is ready to learn new words. The new words you teach should be chosen carefully so that they are easy for your child to say and understand. Short words with only a few different sounds are easiest to say. For example, *ball* and *dog* are easy words, whereas *crocodile* and *sandwich* are more difficult. Simple nouns—words that name familiar objects, animals, or people—are easiest for your child to understand and, therefore, to say. These include words like *nose, cup, cat, eye, boat, mamma,* and *baby.* Other parts of speech—verbs, adjectives, and concepts—are generally too abstract to use as beginning words. As is often the case, there are exceptions. If there is an abstract word such as *up, out,* or *gone* that is particularly meaningful to your child, then of course you should use it.

Table 5.2 contains lists of common words that will help you choose new words to teach. Use the words in this table and the list of words that your child understands but does not say (compiled in Table 5.1) to determine appropriate words to teach your child. We recommend that the first 15–20 words you teach be the names of meaningful common objects and/or familiar animals and people because these are easiest for your child to understand. Words that name food, furniture, clothing, toys, or parts of the body are good object words to teach. One way to recall words to teach is to concentrate on classes of words such as those displayed in Table 5.2. Another way is to name single nouns.

Teaching New Words

When teaching new words, there are a few important points to remember. First, it should be emphasized that it is important to plan each session in advance. Have a word list that includes all the words your child can say and at least 10–15 new ones. Plan more than enough words to teach so that you always have new words to work with during the session. Teaching new words is one way to keep the sessions interesting for your child and keep his or her vocabulary growing.

A general strategy that applies to all the teaching sessions is to begin and finish with easy requests and to present the more difficult or new material during the middle portion of the 12-minute session. By beginning and finishing with easy requests, both a successful start and positive conclusion (and hence, an overall beneficial experience) are more likely to occur. The power of this program rests on that fact that talking must become a highly positive experience. Children with productive-language delays cannot be forced to talk; they must first be enticed and then rewarded for their cooperation.

Start the sessions by rehearsing familiar words to help your child remember what he or she has learned and to begin successfully. This will put both of you in a good mood for the harder words to come. Incidentally, if your child is imitating words easily during the rehearsal, reward

TABLE 5.2
Word List

Body Parts

Easier to Say			Harder to Say
back	knee		arm
ear	neck		chest
eye	nose		finger
foot	toe		leg
hair	tummy		mouth
hand			teeth

Clothing

Easier to Say		Harder to Say	
boot	mitten	belt	shoes
button	pants	buckle	shorts
cap	pocket	dress	skirt
coat	sock	jacket	sneakers
hat		jeans	zipper
		shirt	

Furniture, Household Items, Utensils

Easier to Say		Harder to Say	
bed	light	bag	pillow
cup	pan	bathroom	plate
door	phone	bowl	room
fork	pot	chair	rug
key	soap	clock	sink
knife	tab	closet	spoon
lamp	TV	couch	stairs
	tub	dish	stove
		floor	table
		highchair	wall
		kitchen	window

Animals

Easier to Say		Harder to Say	
bear	duck	bird	monkey
bee	goat	bug	sheep
cat	kitty	fly	turtle
cow	pony	horse	
dog			

Toys

Easier to Say		Harder to Say	
baby	book	balloon	Play Doh
ball	box	block	puzzle
bat	bus	clay	shovel
bike	car	crayon	train
boat		doll	truck
		plane	wagon

TABLE 5.2
Word List
(Continued)

People

baby
daddy
mommy
(names of brothers, sisters, and friends)

Food and Drink

Easier to Say		*Harder to Say*	
butter	meat	apple	jelly
cake	pancake	bread	juice
candy	peanut	cereal	milk
coke	pie	cheese	orange
cookie	raisin	corn	sandwich
gum	tuna	egg	soup
		fish	toast
		ice cream	water

Action Words

Easier to Say		*Harder to Say*	
come	kiss	break	spill
cut	open	brush	splash
eat	pat	clap	stand
fall	pull	climb	stir
go	push	close	throw
hold	read	draw	try
hug	ride	drink	touch
jump	run	dry	turn
	sit	play	walk
		scrub	wash
		shut	wipe
			write

Greetings and Concepts

all done	more
all gone	night-night
bye	on / off
hi	please
in / off	up / down

each imitation with praise and attention, but give a food reward only every second or third time he or she says what you ask (partial reward). This will encourage your child to speak more often and make him or her less likely to forget what has been learned.

After you have spent 2–3 minutes rehearsing well-learned words, go on to teach new words. Ask your child to repeat the new words in the same way that you ask him or her to say familiar words. Make your requests short and simple. For example, if you are teaching the word *doggie,* say: "Dennis, say *doggie.* (Pause.) *Doggie.*" If your child says the whole word *doggie* or any of the sounds in it, reward him or her enthusiastically with food, the toy dog, and praise, and ask him or her to repeat it. When your child is first learning a new word, give food rewards, the object when possible, and praise, even if what he or she says is only partially correct. Children need the encouragement of rewards if they are to continue trying. Also, rewards let children know that they are on the right track. However, once a word has been learned well, reward each repetition with attention and praise, but provide food rewards only every second or third time that the word is spoken. In other words, only use a *partial reward* strategy for the edibles.

In addition, remember to restrict your reward primarily to your child's best efforts. In the beginning, he or she may say only the first sound of the word. Your child may say *duh* rather than *doggie,* for example. Initially, these responses should be rewarded, even though they are not completely correct. However, once you have heard your child say the full word *doggie* a few times, do not provide rewards anymore when your child says *duh.* Give all the help that may be needed, but encourage your child to do the best that he or she can during the teaching session.

Before ending a session, make sure that your child is performing successfully. If your child has not learned to say the words you are working on, go back to the words he or she knows well and end the session on a positive note. It is important that your child start and end a session earning rewards successfully because this helps make the sessions enjoyable and promotes hard work at language learning. If your child has a particularly good session, you can follow it with a larger food reward or a special activity to let him or her know that you are pleased with the session. A glass of juice, a dish of ice cream, or a trip to the playground can be given as a special treat. Parents should be certain to let their child know exactly why he or she is receiving an extra treat.

General Teaching Techniques

To help your child understand the meanings of new words, you should always try to show objects or pictures that represent the words you are trying to teach. For example, if you are teaching the word *spoon,* show your child a real spoon as you say the word and ask him or her to repeat it. Toys can be used to represent words like *car, boat,* and *airplane.* Pictures are good to use when it is not possible to have real objects or toys present. The pictures should be relatively large, clear examples of the words you are teaching. Often it is helpful to paste individual pictures on separate sheets of paper so they can be shown one at a time. If your child is shown several pictures together at once, he or she may get confused and distracted. You might even create your child's own looseleaf picture-word book. However, parents should exercise caution because sometimes children become more interested in turning magazine pages than practicing new words. Nevertheless, objects and pictures are important teaching props that help children connect words with the objects they name, so they should be used. Unless children understand these connections, their speech may not be useful or meaningful to them.

To help your child understand action words, it is useful to perform the actions yourself, act them out with a doll, or display clear pictures of the actions. For example, when teaching *sit* and *stand,* you can sit down as you say *sit* and stand up as you say *stand.* Have your child and a doll perform the actions, too. Similarly, a picture of a child swimming or jumping would help illustrate these action verbs. Props and techniques for use during the teaching session are suggested at the end of this chapter. Try to use them whenever possible because they will make the sessions more interesting and it will be easier for your child to understand the meanings of the words he or she is learning to say.

You should be aware that teaching props, like books, may distract your child and make it difficult for him or her to attend during the sessions. For example, a child shown a new doll for the first time may be more interested in playing with the doll than in talking about it. To avoid this problem, let your child play with a new object briefly before it is used during the teaching sessions. Your child is less likely to be distracted by a familiar object than a novel one. To minimize distractions, try to use only one teaching prop at a time and keep the others out of sight. It is often less distracting to keep the objects in a bag and bring them out as you are ready to use them.

A Comment About Articulation

When children first begin to speak, they usually find it difficult to say words clearly and distinctly. They omit or add sounds to words and they slur sounds together. These problems are common to virtually *all* children when they are learning to talk and should not be a major concern when your child is just beginning the training program. As long as you can understand what your child is saying, do not be worried if his or her speech is not completely clear. It is more important to focus on teaching new words than to worry about how clearly they are said during the beginning phases of this program. As your child practices talking, his or her speech should become clearer naturally.

The issue of articulation difficulties is raised here because some parents become concerned that their child's first words are almost correct, but not fully correct, even though the child may use them appropriately. The purpose of this section is to urge you not to be overly concerned about articulation during the initial phases of this program. It is far more important to create a willingness to use words, even almost correct words, at this stage than to risk a breakdown in your child's progress by emphasizing better articulation. An excessive emphasis on articulation too early in the program can turn the productive language training sessions into a negative, rather than positive, experience.

If your child is still articulating words poorly when using two- and three-word sentences, then articulation may require some special attention. Several techniques for dealing with articulation problems are described at the end of this manual in Appendix A. If the techniques in Appendix A are not sufficient to improve your child's speech, then he or she should be evaluated by a certified speech therapist. The speech therapist may be able to identify the cause of specific problems and provide recommendations for dealing with them.

GENERALIZING BEYOND
THE TEACHING SESSIONS

Once your child has learned to say words and responds to the majority of your requests for speech in the sessions, it is important to extend (generalize) his or her talking to other times of the day. The teaching sessions enable your child to learn new words efficiently and to practice saying them. However, your child must also learn to talk outside the sessions in order to make this language useful. There are several ways to encourage your child to use productive language for communication outside the teaching sessions. These include asking questions, real-world contingencies (situations) where your child must use a word to get something, and informal language stimulation.

ASKING QUESTIONS:
AN ESSENTIAL FEATURE

Why Should Parents Ask Questions?

Teaching your child to answer questions is not only an effective way to encourage talking outside the sessions, but it is virtually essential for communication to develop. Without the ability to answer questions, verbal communication would be largely one-sided. Your child would either respond to your question "Who's this?" with the answer "Who's this?" or only talk about the few things he or she chose to express at any moment. Unfortunately, speaking a few words only when a child wishes is one of the principal reasons that parents seek this program in the first place.

Answering questions is a more difficult task than simply saying words. To imitate a word, children have to match or copy a sound that they hear. We are not suggesting that this is an easy task. Your child must receive a sound using hearing and immediately re-create that sound using another skill—talking. Imitation alone is not enough for communication to develop because your child must be able to generate speech spontaneously in order to express thoughts and needs. Imitation reflects someone else's thoughts or needs, not necessarily your child's own ideas.

To answer a question, a child not only must receive information using one ability and produce a response using a diffrent skill, but the information itself must be transformed or changed before a response is produced. For example, if a girl is shown a ball and asked, "What's this?" she should not answer "What's this?" but should say *ball*. The question must be "processed" or thought about, the correct answer must be retrieved from the child's memory, and the appropriate response must be produced using speech without an external model for the sound. Not only will asking questions teach your child the give and take of verbal communication, but it will increase the likelihood of spontaneous talking. It appears that a child who is accustomed to answering questions may be more likely to label objects spontaneously as well because answering questions provides practice with retrieving the correct words from his or her memory. The main point of this section is to emphasize that learning to answer questions is an extremely important skill for the development of productive language.

Answering questions should be taught during the training sessions as often as possible, but questions should be asked at other times of the day as well. An excellent first question to teach your child to answer is "What's this?" In fact, if you have difficulty rephrasing your comments in the form of questions to your child, you could do well to remember only one: " What's this?" It is a question that can be asked of most things in your child's environment, particularly the concrete nouns that are emphasized in the beginning of the program. By repeating the questions and rewording the correct answers, your child will come to know the meaning of "What's this?"

An Illustration

A look at the teaching session during which Jonathan's mother taught him the transition from imitation to answering questions can serve as a good model. Jonathan's mother selected familiar objects that he could recognize and whose names he could imitate. She chose a cup and a ball and put one of the objects—the ball—out of sight.

Mother:	(Holds the cup in front of Jonathan.) "Jonathan. What's this?"
Jonathan:	(Reaches for the cup, but says nothing.)
Mother:	(Holds the cup in front of Jonathan, but out of reach.) "Jonathan. What's this?"
Jonathan:	(Still says nothing.)
Mother:	"Cup. Jonathan, say cup."
Jonathan:	"Cup."
Mother:	"Good boy, Jonathan." (Places a raisin in his mouth.) "Cup, Jonathan."
Jonathan:	"Cup." (Reaches for the cup.)
Mother:	"Good, Jonathan. This is a cup." (Places a raisin in his mouth.) "What's this?" (Holds the cup in front of Jonathan.)
Jonathan:	"Cup." (Reaches for the cup again.)
Mother:	"Excellent. This is a cup." (This time she gives the cup to Jonathan and places a raisin in it while he holds the cup.)
Jonathan:	(Takes the raisin out, eats it, and holds the cup by the handle.)
Mother:	(Gently removes the cup and holds it up.) "What's this?"
Jonathan:	"Cup."
Mother:	"Good boy." (Holds the cup up again.) "What's this?"
Jonathan:	"Cup." (Reaches for the cup.)
Mother:	"Excellent." (Gives Jonathan the cup and places a raisin in his mouth.)

Jonathan's mother then removed the cup, put it in a bag, and brought out the ball. She repeated the same procedure with the ball until Jonathan could say *ball* without hesitation when shown the ball and asked "What's this?" Next, she decided that she would alternate between the ball and the cup. She presented the ball and asked "What's this?" Jonathan answered correctly and was rewarded. Then she presented the cup and asked the same question. Again, Jonathan was correct and was given praise and a raisin. She continued to alternate back and forth between the cup and the ball until Jonathan named each object correctly three times.

If any of Jonathan's answers were wrong, his mother would have prompted the correct answer and repeated the questions until a correct answer was produced spontaneously. She used this technique with other familiar objects. In each case, she taught Jonathan to respond to "What's this?" with each object alone. Then she rehearsed the question for that object along with the other objects that Jonathan learned to label. After this first session, Jonathan's mother regularly rehearsed responding to "What's this?" for all the objects that Jonathan learned to label. It did not take long for Jonathan to understand the meaning of the question "What's this?" using this procedure.

A second question that Jonathan's mother taught him to answer was "Who's this?" The procedure for teaching answers to this question was the same as the one described for "What's this?" She followed the steps that were just described, but used real people and their pictures instead of objects. Learning to answer "Who's this?" correctly helped Jonathan to say the names of people on his own, outside the teaching sessions.

By answering questions frequently, children gain experience processing or thinking about verbal information and generating the right answers. These experiences set the stage for the communicative use of speech. They help children to talk normally. Therefore, "What's this?," "Who's this?," and other questions should be asked both during and outside of the teaching sessions. It is extremely important to turn imitation of a word into a spontaneous statement, the way that Jonathan's mother did. Once a child understands the meaning of "What's this?" the question should be asked routinely for all newly learned words as soon as they are imitated correctly. In other words, have your child name the word through imitation first followed immediately by the question "What's this?" just as Jonathan's mother did.

SETTING REAL-WORLD CONTINGENCIES

One way to encourage your child to use productive language outside the teaching sessions is to make specific requests for words at other times of the day. Start by selecting five or six situations in the course of a normal day where your child can be encouraged to use the words that have been learned. Some possibilities are:

1. If your child is thirsty and knows how to name or ask for a drink, require him or her to say *juice* or *more* before giving the beverage.
2. If your child wants to go outside to play, insist that he or she say *open* before opening the door.
3. Ask your child to say *up* before getting him or her from the crib in the morning or before lifting him or her onto your lap.
4. Ask your child to name a toy before you let him or her play with it.

For example, if your child is able, require that he or she say *truck* before receiving a toy truck.

Follow the same rules in these situations as in the teaching sessions. Tell your child what you want him or her to say and wait for an acceptable response before giving the desired object or outcome. You can help your child by repeating the word as a reminder, but once the request for the word is made, it is essential to withhold the desired goal or naturally occurring reward until the correct word is spoken. Do not "give in" by rewarding a gesture or scream, because you will encourage those unwanted actions.

Just as you carefully selected the first words to use in the teaching sessions, you should carefully select the situations during the day in which you require your child to speak in order to get the object. Be sure that he or she can say the appropriate words and insist that your child say them. Do not ask your child to say *out* if you are in a hurry to leave and cannot calmly wait for a response. In other words, make sure that your child is able to respond to the request and that you have the time to encourage speaking. In addition, be certain that you are prepared to withhold the reward if your child does not respond correctly. Therefore, you must be willing to keep your child in the house if he or she refuses to say *out* for you. Do not set a contingency for productive language in a natural context unless you can follow through with these conditions.

Requesting productive language outside the sessions is one of the most effective ways to help your child use speech to communicate. Try to be consistent with the words that you request and try to ask your child to speak as frequently as possible. Other family members should do the same. They can help your child learn to communicate with others and can provide more opportunities to practice talking. In fact, the help of other family members is important for the success of the language program. Demands for speech must be made consistently if language learning is to progress. If some people require that your child speak and others do not, your child may get confused and not know what to do. Inconsistency of treatment is likely to delay your child's progress with talking. However, if all family members follow the same rules, your child will soon learn that he or she must speak to get what is desired. Thus, your child will talk more often and progress will be more rapid if there is consistency of treatment.

INFORMAL LANGUAGE STIMULATION

There are many times during the day when it is possible to talk to your child and provide informal language stimulation. Speaking to your child is important because the more language that he or she hears, the more likely he or she is to learn new words and speak independently. This is particularly important once the productive language sessions have begun. Obviously, your child has heard language in the past; the main difference is that now more than ever, he or she is encouraged to speak. Your child's growing ability to talk will make him or her more receptive to the language that you use.

One easy approach is to talk to your child in simple language about your daily activities. For example, while you are cooking, say "Pour in the milk" or "I'm, stirring soup." While gardening, say "I'm digging" or "Pick the flowers." If you begin to think that you sound like a sports announcer giving a play-by-play description of a football game, then you know you are doing the right thing. In addition to simple descriptions, it is helpful to point out new sounds and objects to your child when they occur. When the phone rings, say "Hear the phone ringing," or when a dog barks, say "Hear the dog." Teach your child to attend to the tick of a clock, the splash of running water, and the hum of a passing car. In short, focus your child's attention on sounds, point out and name new objects, and above all, praise and reward your child's attempts to speak back to you.

Speak to your child whenever you can, but the most important thing is to encourage and reward your child's speech in these informal situations. If your child repeats words after you or answers a question, praise him or her enthusiastically. Whenever your child speaks, listen to what he or she says and always respond. This may be difficult in large or busy households where a child's attempts at talking can go unnoticed. Thus, parents of large families should make an extra effort to respond to their child's attempts at talking. Keep in mind that your child's speech delay is a temporary phenomenon that will improve soon.

The intense interest in language that is encouraged in this manual is appropriate during a developmental period in which children normally begin to talk. It is highly likely that when your child first began to walk alone, both your attention and your child's were focused appropriately on walking. A central developmental accomplishment during the second and third years of life is learning to talk, a task that also deserves your enthusiastic attention. The development of talking is important for your child's future linguistic, intellectual, and social development. However, it is unnecessary to emphasize productive language at later periods in development as your child becomes a competent speaker, just as it is unnecessary to maintain intense interest in your child's motor development after he or she has learned to walk and run.

As we have stated repeatedly, the goal of the language teaching program is to help your child use productive language spontaneously for communication with others. Speaking to your child, listening to what he or she says, and rewarding his or her own efforts at talking are important ways to help your child achieve the communicative use of productive language.

EVENTS AND PROPS TO ENCOURAGE TALKING

In this final section, events and props that can be used in the language sessions are presented. For example, there are suggestions for teaching each class of words in Table 5.2, including events and props for teaching body parts, names of furniture, and toys. Ways to help your child generalize or expand the use of words to other times during the day after he or she has learned to say the words in the teaching sessions are also presented. These suggestions are listed for each class of words under the heading *Generalization*. A sample teaching plan illustrating how one mother planned a teaching session for her child is presented in Table 5.3 to help you plan sessions for your child.

This portion of the manual can be used as a reference. Look through it when you are deciding how to teach specific words to your child. Usually, you will need to use only one of the events or props in a teaching session, and you can use the same situation 2 or 3 days in a row. Change to a new event or prop if your child becomes bored with the old one or if your child has learned the words and is ready to practice saying them in a new context. Changing contexts will help your child understand the meanings of the words he or she is learning to say. For example, it is important that your child be able to name body parts on dolls and on pictures as well as on people. If he or she can name body parts in all these contexts, it is clear that your child understands and has generalized the meanings of the words.

TABLE 5.3

Child's Name _____   Date _____

Teacher _____

Sample Word List

Familiar Words & Sentences	No. Responses	Familiar Words & Sentences	No. Responses
1 eye		mouth	
2 nose		ear	
3 cookie		juice	
4 cup		apple	
5 shoe		milk	
6 ball		spoon	
7 doggie		sock	
8 hi		pants	
9		hat	
10		car	
11		truck	
12		book	
13		kitty	
14		duck	
15		baby	
16		bye bye	
17		up	
18			
19			
20			
21			
22			
23			
24			
25			
26			
27			
28			
29			
30			

Total   Single Words   _____   Different   Single Words _____
            2-Word Sentences _____   2-Word Sentences _____
            3-Word Sentences _____   3-Word Sentences _____

Keep in mind that not all of these activities will be appropriate for your child. A variety of situations and games are presented so that you may choose activities that match your child's level of development.

Games to Play

Body Parts

1. Point to your own body parts as you say the words and ask your child to repeat them. You can also use your child, another family member, a doll, a stuffed animal, or a large picture of a face or body from a magazine to illustrate body parts.

2. Draw a face or an entire person with your child. Ask your child to name each body part before you add it to the picture.
3. Make a face or an entire person puzzle by pasting a large magazine picture onto a piece of heavy cardboard. Cut the picture out into four or five large, simple shapes with one body part per piece. Make the puzzle with your child during the sessions. Ask him or her to name the body parts on each piece *before* giving the piece to put in the puzzle.
4. Pretend to give a doll a bath and have your child name each body part on the doll as he or she washes it with a small sponge and dries it with a cloth.

Clothing

1. Point to examples of clothing as you say the words and ask your child to repeat them. Use your own clothes, your child's clothes, and pictures of clothes from magazines as examples. Mail-order catalogs are often good sources of clothing pictures.
2. Dress and undress a doll. Ask your child to name each piece of clothing *before* you give it to him or her to put on the doll and as he or she takes it off the doll.
3. Using a small box or container as a basin, pretend to wash a doll's clothes and put them out to dry. Ask your child to name each piece of clothing *before* you give it to him or her to wash and *before* each piece is put out to dry.

Furniture, Household Items, Toys

1. Point to furniture in the room and show household items and toys as you use the appropriate name. Ask your child to repeat the words after you. Stuffed animals can be used to teach animal names, and pictures can be used if real objects are not available.
2. Pretend to wash and dry some dishes and pots. Ask your child to name each item *before* you give it to him or her to wash or dry.
3. If you have a doll house and furniture, ask your child to name rooms and furniture *before* you give him or her the objects to put in the house.

People

1. Ask other family members to participate in the sessions, or use photographs when teaching people's names.
2. Have a second parent conduct the sessions on occasion.

Food and Drink

1. Show your child actual food and drink items or clear pictures from magazines. Say the words and ask your child to repeat them.

2. Require your child to name the food rewards used during the sessions.
3. Use Play-Doh to make and name pretend food with your child. For example, make and label pretend cookies, pancakes, carrots, or peas and pretend to cook them. (Be certain that your child understands the concept of pretend activities before trying this game.)

Action Words

1. One of the best ways to teach action words is to perform the actions while you and your child say the appropriate words. Dolls can also be used to model different actions. When teaching an action word, start with an action that your child already can do. Name the action as you perform it or as you act it out with a doll and then ask your child to say the word and perform the action too. For example, say *clapping* as you clap your hands. Ask your child to say *clapping* and guide his or her hands through the motions of clapping. Repeat this until your child easily repeats the word *clapping* each time you request it.
2. For some action words, it will help you to use an object when demonstrating the action. For example, a pull toy can be used to demonstrate *pulling,* a spoon and a cup to demonstrate *stirring,* and a sponge and doll or dishes to demonstrate *washing.* Name the action as you perform it, ask your child to repeat the appropriate word, and then let your child perform the action. Eventually, the opportunity to perform the action should become contingent (dependent) upon saying the appropriate word.

Greetings and Concepts

1. Use a doll to teach the meanings of the words *hi, bye,* and *night.* Ask your child to say *hi* to the doll when you first introduce it into the teaching sessions and to say *bye* to the doll when you put it away. Pretend to put the doll to sleep and ask your child to say *night.*
2. To teach the word *more,* pour a small amount of juice into the glass and let your child drink it. Then ask him or her to say *more.* Only after repeating the word *more* should you pour more juice into the glass for your child to drink. Continue to insist that your child say *more* before giving more juice. Introduce the words *all gone* when there is no more juice left. Show your child the empty juice container and say *all gone.* Ask him or her to repeat the phrase *all gone,* but accept a one-sysllable approximation such as *gone* at this point in the program.
3. When teaching the words *up* and *down* begin with the word *up.* Demonstrate the meaning of *up* to your child by saying *up* and then

immediately pick him or her up. Repeat this three or four times. Then ask your child to say *up*. Pick him or her up immediately if he or she says *up* or something close to it like *uh*. If your child does not say *up*, demonstrate the word a few more times. Again, ask your child to say *up*. If he or she still does not respond, use another child or doll to model saying *up*. Ask the model to say *up* and pick the model up immediately after saying it. Again, ask your child to say *up* and pick him or her up only if he or she responds appropriately. When your child consistently repeats the word *up*, you can begin to teach *down*. First, demonstrate the word by holding your child on your lap, saying *down*, and then immediately placing him or her on the floor. Repeat this three of four times. Then ask your child to say *down* before you place him or her on the floor. If your child does not imitate the word *down*, use another child to model what to do. When *up* and *down* are repeated consistently, ask your child to say *up* and *down* in alternation until both words are spoken easily. This *up–down* game can be made more interesting by lifting your child high in the air with enthusiasm and singing the words *up* and *down*. Remember to pick up or put down your child immediately when he or she says the appropriate word.

You may also want to use a doll or some other object to model the movements. When your child says *up*, pick up the doll or toy; when he or she says *down*, put it down on the floor or table. A toy airplane can take off into the sky while saying *up* and land on the runway when saying *down*. Practicing *up* and *down* with toys should be started only after your child clearly understands how to say *up* and *down* to describe his or her own actions.

4. Teach your child to say *on* and *off* as you dress and undress a doll. Begin teaching with the word *on*. Demonstrate the meaning of the word by saying *on* as you put a hat or a sock on a doll. Then ask your child to say *on* before either of you puts another article of clothing on the doll. Use another person to model saying *on* if your child does not understand what to do. When your child consistently repeats the word *on*, you can begin to teach *off*. Demonstrate the meaning of the word by saying *off* before you take a hat or sock off a doll. Then ask your child to say *off* before either of you takes another article of clothing off the doll. Use another person as a model, if necessary, to help your child understand what to do. When *off* is consistently repeated, ask your child to say *on* and *off* in alternation as you dress and undress a doll. Continue practicing both words together until your child uses them correctly in the sessions.

EVENTS FOR GENERALIZING
OUTSIDE THE SESSIONS

This section on generalization differs from the previous one, Games to Play, in at least one important respect. The games are practice activities that use pretend play and props during the teaching sessions. They set the stage for generalization. On the other hand, the generalization activities represent the real thing. They contain a list of activities and situations that actually occur in your child's everyday life. Their function is to encourage your child to link talking with everyday activities. In each case, an effort should be made to make the naturally occurring activity (e.g., juice for a snack) contingent upon the proper use of productive language (the word *juice*, in this case) by your child.

These generalization procedures facilitate productive language in two ways. First, they provide an opportunity to rehearse familiar words in your child's vocabulary; second, they allow you to present objects and actions contingent upon productive language in both the teaching sessions and the natural home context. The key to contingent presentation of consequences is to have your child name the object *before* you give it to him or her. Also, as mentioned earlier, you must be willing to withhold the object if resistance occurs. These generalization procedures are designed to add meaning to the words in your child's vocabulary and to increase the tendency to use productive language for communication. By presenting many objects contingently in these planned situations, your child will learn to announce his or her thoughts and needs verbally. Moreover, practice with the contingent presentation of objects outside the teaching sessions will help your child to learn that interaction with others requires giving as well as taking. This verbal give and take will help to reduce the noncompliant and resistant behavior that often accompanies speech delays.

Body Parts

1. Practice naming body parts while bathing your child and while helping him or her to wash up before and after meals.
2. Practice naming body parts while dressing and undressing.
3. Sing songs with your child that emphasize names of body parts. Consult Appendix B for a listing of children's songs that you might use.

Clothing

1. Practice naming clothing while dressing and undressing your child.
2. Require your child to say *coat, hat, socks,* and *shoes,* for example,

before letting him or her put them on or *before* you put them on.
3. Practice naming clothing while folding laundry or while looking through a clothes closet with your child.

Furniture, Household Items, Toys

1. Practice naming furniture, rooms, toys, and other household items as you walk around the house with your child.
2. Require your child to say *TV* before turning the television on.
3. Require your child to say *light* before letting him or her flick the light switch.
4. Require your child to name a toy *before* being allowed to play with it.
5. Practice naming utensils and dishes as you set the table, eat a meal, and clean up afterwards.

People

1. Encourage your child to name people when they visit.
2. Make a point to allow your child to greet and talk to the letter or newspaper carrier.
3. After returning from work, have your child tell the second parent the new words learned each day.

Food and Drink

1. Require your child to name foods eaten outside the teaching sessions. Between-meal snacks (e.g., juice, milk, crackers, cookies, fruit, and desserts) are good foods to use. Ask your child to name the snack and give it only if he or she responds appropriately to your requests. This is one of the most powerful natural contingencies that can be presented, so be certain to present the treat only if the proper word or word approximation is used. You must be willing to withhold the snack if your child refuses to comply.
2. Practice naming the foods your child is eating during a meal.
3. Practice naming foods as you shop in the supermarket and as you put the groceries away at home.

Action Words

1. Describe what you and your child are doing during the course of the day.
2. As you look through picture books with your child, talk about the actions that are occurring as well as the objects in the pictures.
3. Sing songs with your child that describe simple actions that you can perform as you sing. Consult Appendix B for a list of appropriate children's songs.

Greetings and Concepts

1. It is important to use the words *hi, bye, night, more, gone* or *all gone, up, down, on,* and *off* appropriately in context whenever possible during the day. The meanings of these words are most clearly taught in real-world situations outside the teaching sessions. These concepts are more abstract and difficult for children to understand than the names of objects, and it appears to be necessary to provide many examples of different situations.
2. Require your child to say *more* before giving another serving of a snack or treat.
3. Require your child to say *up* before picking him or her up and *down* before putting him or her down. Usually, there is no pressing need to pick your child up, so it is easy to wait until he or she says *up* appropriately. Moreover, children are often content to be held for a few minutes, making it appropriate to request the word *down* after briefly holding your child. Thus, saying *up* and *down* is an ideal natural contingency to promote the generalization of talking, which can be practiced frequently.
4. Practice the words *on* and *off* as you dress and undress your child.

6

Teaching Two-Word Sentences

INTRODUCTION

The second major goal of the productive language program is to teach children to say simple, two-word sentences like *more juice, open door,* or *baby's shoe.* Combining familiar words to form simple two-word sentences is a major event in the development of children's talking. Children who can say two-word sentences communicate more effectively and show the potential for learning more complex forms of talking.

Children without delayed speech usually begin to put two words together spontaneously and without instruction when they acquire a vocabulary of about 60 words. The reasons for this change in development are not well understood, but this fact is useful for judging a child's readiness to learn two-word sentences. Some children with productive-language delays also begin to use two-word sentences spontaneously when they are able to say about 60 different words. However, other speech-delayed children need more help in moving from single words to combining words into sentences. In either case, the teaching sessions will help to encourage this new phase of language production. For children who begin to combine words on their own, the teaching sessions can help to solidify and expand this new skill. For children who need more help in learning to produce two-word sentences, the teaching sessions can provide the necessary practice and encouragement for progress with talking.

The main objective of this chapter is to describe ways to teach two-word sentences during the productive language sessions. Simple two-word sentences are learned during the teaching sessions first, and

TABLE 6.1
Sample Word List

Objects		People	Actions	Other
bus	baby	mommy	eat	more
book	block	daddy	sit	please
truck	house	Bobby	drink	hi
car	bed	Susie	play	bye
ball	light	grandma	go	all gone
bottle	cup	grandpa	push	hot
berry	juice		close	no
peanut	milk		kiss	mine
cheese	cookie		open	night-night
bath	cracker		down	
hair	nose		up	
car	eyes		out	
knee	mouth		off	
door	toes			
potty	tummy			
shoe	sock			
brush	doggie			
soap	cat			
cookie	chair			
blanket	phone			
hat				

generalized outside of the session to events in daily life later. The production of two-word sentences is a major landmark in the development of speech that deserves special attention in the teaching sessions.

Three criteria can be used to determine whether your child is ready to begin this part of the teaching program. First, your child should be able to say at least 60 different single words, and these words should be of different types. They should include the names of objects (e.g., *car, spoon*), people (e.g., mommy, daddy), actions (e.g.,*eat, go*) and concepts (e.g., *up, out*). Second, your child should be able to use words easily; he or she should be able to produce about 30 words during a 12-minute session. Third, your child should be using many of these words appropriately outside of the teaching sessions and at other times during the day. For example, he or she should be using *car* to label a toy car and *open* to ask for help in opening a door or jar. If your child's productive language skills fulfill these three criteria, then he or she is ready to learn to produce two-word sentences. However, if these three criteria are not met, do not begin this part of the program yet. Instead, you should continue to focus on expanding your child's single-word vocabulary and practicing familiar words during the teaching sessions. You should also continue to encourage the use of single words outside the teaching sessions.

TABLE 6.2
Form for Preparing Two-Word Sentences

Before reading on, use the appropriate spaces to list the words your child can say.

Word List			
Objects	*People*	*Actions*	*Other*
————	————	————	————	————
————	————	————	————	————
————	————	————	————	————
————	————	————	————	————
————	————	————	————	————
————	————	————	————	————
————	————	————	————	————
————	————	————	————	————
————	————	————	————	————
————	————	————	————	————
————	————	————	————	————

THE USE OF TWO-WORD SENTENCES

When children first begin to put words together, they often talk about similar things. They make requests such as *more juice, more cookie,* and they greet and say goodbye to people (e.g., *hi mommy, bye daddy*). They describe events and may say *go car* or *baby down,* and they talk about objects and their owners and may say *dolly shoe* or *Adam truck.* Each of these ideas is communicated through the use of a simple two-word sentence. This chapter discusses ways to teach your child to combine familiar words to form these different types of simple two-word utterances. In order to plan the sessions, you will need a current list of the words your child knows. Compile the words into four categories: objects, people, actions, and other. Table 6.1 contains a sample word list divided into these four categories. Table 6.2 is provided so that you can make lists of objects, people, actions, and other words for your own child.

Choosing Two-Word Sentences

Before beginning the teaching sessions, you should think carefully about the kinds of two-word sentences you want to teach. The most important point to remember is that the sentences you choose should describe events that are common and meaningful to your child. By using words that your child already knows and events that he or she understands, the task of putting two-words together will be simplified.

There are several ways to gain an idea of which events might be familiar to your child. First, think about the kinds of events that occur regularly in the child's daily life. Activities like eating meals, taking a bath, dressing and undressing, or taking a nap are familiar events for most children under 3. Two-word sentences describing any of these events are likely to be meaningful to most of them. Second, watch your child play to observe the kinds of things that he or she may act out. It is common for young children to engage in pretend play using familiar daily events, particularly when they are playing with dolls. They will pretend to feed a doll with a bottle or spoon, dress and undress the doll, and put the doll to bed. Third, notice the words your child already uses. Think about the kinds of events that his or her words describe. Look at your word list in Table 6.2. You will probably find words associated with eating (e.g., *bottle, juice, cracker, eat, drink*), dressing (e.g., *shoes, sock, tummy, brush, off*), sleeping (*night-night, bed, blanket*), and other common activities (e.g., *go, car, out*). These three sources of information—common real-life events, events acted out in play, and current words—should give you a good idea of the kinds of events that are most meaningful to your child. The two-word sentences that you prepare to teach should describe these meaningful events.

To help you create a list of two-word sentences appropriate for your child, we have organized a sample list in Table 6.3. These sentences are listed under several headings and are presented from relatively common to less common sets. The first list is organized according to action events that consist of *action-object* sentences (e.g., *eat cookie* and *wash hands*) and *doer-action* sentences (e.g., *mommy eats* and *daddy washes*). Sentences that can be created by combining many familiar words with the requests *more* and *please* (e.g., *more juice* and *cookie please*) are easy sentences to learn. Because requests combine easily into familiar two-word sentences and are redundant, your child can focus his or her effort on speaking a longer statement rather than learning new words. Sentences that combine the greetings *hello* (or *hi*) and *goodbye* (or *bye*) with familiar persons and animals can be used frequently. These naturally occurring simple sentences (e.g., *hi grandpa* and *bye doggie*) can also encourage your child to talk to other persons. Sentences that announce possession by combining a *name and object* (e.g., *daddy's car* and *kitty's nose*) are

TABLE 6.3
Sample List of Two-Word Sentences

Actions

Action Word + Object Word	Doer Word + Action Word
close door	mommy closes
close box	John closes
eat cookie	mommy eats
eat toast	daddy eats
push truck	doggie eats
push car	kitty eats
wash hands	mommy pushes
wash ears	John pushes
wash mouth	daddy washes
	mommy washes
	John washes
	dolly sits
	mommy sits

Object Word + Please	More + Object Word
juice please	more juice
cookie please	more cookies
TV please	more TV
toys please	more toys

Greetings	Possessives
Greeting & Name	Name + Object
hi mommy	Adam's shirt
bye mommy	Adam's shoe
hi doggie	Adam's nose
bye kitty	Adam's eye
hi grandma	doggie's mouth
hi grandpa	kitty's ear
bye grandma	mommy's hair
bye grandpa	mommy's dress
hi daddy	daddy's car
bye daddy	daddy's hand

Concepts

Object Word + Concept Word	Action Word + Concept Word
ball up	sit up
ball down	sit down
sock on	stand up
sock off	walk up
shirt on	walk down
shirt off	climb up
hat on	climb down
hat off	push on
spoon in (a cup)	push off
toy out (of a toy box)	turn on
foot in (a shoe)	turn off
hand out (of a mitten)	walk in
	walk out
	come in
	come out

TABLE 6.4
Two-Word Sentences Appropriate for Your Child

1. _____ _____	19. _____ _____
2. _____ _____	20. _____ _____
3. _____ _____	21. _____ _____
4. _____ _____	22. _____ _____
5. _____ _____	23. _____ _____
6. _____ _____	24. _____ _____
7. _____ _____	25. _____ _____
8. _____ _____	26. _____ _____
9. _____ _____	27. _____ _____
10. _____ _____	28. _____ _____
11. _____ _____	29. _____ _____
12. _____ _____	30. _____ _____
13. _____ _____	31. _____ _____
14. _____ _____	32. _____ _____
15. _____ _____	33. _____ _____
16. _____ _____	34. _____ _____
17. _____ _____	35. _____ _____
18. _____ _____	36. _____ _____

also relatively common. Less common, but appropriate, sentences to use include *object-concept* combinations (e.g., *hat on* and *sock off* and *action-concept* sentences (e.g., *sit down* and *stand up*).

You can use Tables 6.1, 6.2, and 6.3 to create two-word sentences that are appropriate and unique to your own child's productive language level. These sentences may be listed in Table 6.4.

An Illustration

Think about how you can plan a teaching session around an eating event. Select a specific event to be described such as feeding a doll. The props needed for the session include a doll, a cookie, and a toy bottle. In addition, you will need the list of words that your child currently knows how to say. Before beginning the session, use your child's word list to make up the two-word sentences about eating that you plan to teach. For example, if your child can say *baby, juice, bottle, drink, eat,* and *cookie,* you can combine these words to form two-word sentences about eating like *baby's bottle, drink juice, eat cookie, baby's cookie,* and *drink bottle.* Have four or five sentences ready before beginning the session. Try to use sentences made up only of words your child already knows, particularly when you are just starting to teach two-word sentences. The main point is to make it easier for your child to say two-word sentences.

Once you have made up your list of two-word sentences, you are ready to begin the session. Sit opposite your child so he or she can see your face clearly, remove all distractions, and have the props and food reward you plan to use close at hand. Begin by rehearsing *single words* that your child has learned to say recently to insure that the session starts successfully. If your child is responding easily during the rehearsal, do not reward every correct response with food. Instead, reward each spoken word with praise and attention, but give a food reward only every third or fourth time he or she speaks appropriately. This partial reward will encourage your child to speak more often and remember what he or she has learned.

After you have spent a few minutes rehearsing single words, go on to teach a few of the two-word sentences you have planned. The techniques used for teaching two-word sentences are the same as those used for teaching single words. For example, to teach *eat raisin*, Adam's mother used raisins and a doll as props and made her requests for speech short and simple.

Mother: (Pretending to feed the doll a raisin.) "Eat raisin. Adam, say eat raisin."
Adam: "Raisin."
Mother: "Look at my mouth, Adam. Eat raisin. Say eat raisin."
Adam: "Raisin."
Mother: "Good boy. You said raisin." (She gives Adam a raisin as a reward.)

Adam had trouble saying both words together, so his mother tried a different strategy. She decided to ask Adam to say the two words separately, one right after the other. Then she asked Adam to say the words closer and closer in time until he could say both words together clearly.

Mother: "Eat. Adam, say eat."
Adam: "Eat."
Mother: "Good boy, Adam. Say raisin."
Adam: "Raisin."
Mother: "Good Adam. Say eat."
Adam: "Eat."
Mother: "Raisin."
Adam: "Raisin."
Mother: "Eat."
Adam: "Eat."
Mother: "Raisin."

Adam: "Raisin."
Mother: "Eat raisin."
Adam: "Ee raisin."
Mother: "Good boy. You said eat raisin." (Gives him a raisin.)
          "Eat raisin."
Adam: "Ee raisin."
Mother: "Good boy. You said eat raisin." (She smiles and gives
          him another raisin.)

Adam's mother rehearsed *eat raisin* four more times so that Adam could practice saying it clearly. She taught him three other two-word sentences *(baby's raisin, baby's bottle,* and *drink bottle)* and ended the session by rehearsing single words.

Articulation Difficulties

There are at least two lessons to be learned from Adam's teaching session with his mother. First, children often have difficulty saying two words together, even if they can say each of the words separately. Adam's mother used a technique to encourage two-word sentences that is frequently successful. She asked Adam to say *eat* and *raisin* separately. Then she proceeded to shorten the amount of time between his imitation of *eat* and *raisin* until he said one right after the other. She was able to encourage Adam to imitate her more quickly each time by increasing the tempo of her requests.

A second lesson is that children often have difficulty articulating words clearly when they are beginning to say two-word sentences. They may omit sounds from words, like the *t* from *eat* as Adam did, or slur the two words together. Difficulties with articulation may occur when learning to combine two words, even if the child has no difficulty saying each of the words alone. Like Adam, they may say *eat* and *raisin* clearly as single words, but pronounce *ee raisin* when they have to put the two words together. Similarly, it is important to know that children often omit the *s* sound on the ends of words. For example, sentences using possessives, formed by adding *'s* to a word, may be hard to say initially. A child may say *baby nose* instead of *baby's nose,* for example. Children omit the *s* sound because it is hard to say and because they do not understand that it is necessary for indicating that the nose belongs to the baby. The use of *s* to represent possession is a rule of grammar that is too difficult for young children to understand. Therefore, if your child omits the final *s,* as in *baby nose,* treat it as a correct response until his or her language is more developed. However, it is important for you to say the final *s* when expressing possession so that your child will hear proper language, even if he or she does not imitate it at this time.

Articulation difficulties are common and should not be a major concern when your child is first beginning to put words together. As long as you can understand what your child is saying, continue to teach new words and word combinations. As your child gains practice talking, his or her speech should become clearer.

Some children have difficulties with articulation that may, in fact, require special attention. However, it is best to wait until your child is using longer sentences before becoming overly concerned. The techniques described in Appendix A, Articulation Problems, can be adapted to help your child say two-word sentences more clearly. If these techniques are not sufficient to improve your child's speech, evaluation by a speech therapist is recommended.

Events for the Teaching Sessions

Other kinds of events that can be used as a basis for the teaching sessions are listed at the end of this chapter. These include events like bathing a doll, putting a doll to bed, and having a tea party. Specific sentences are provided for you to teach during the sessions. Use the examples on this list only if they seem relevant to your child. If other events not listed seem more meaningful, do not hesitate to use them in the teaching sessions. Also, do not restrict yourself to teaching the specific sentences listed. These sentences represent only a few of the many possible word combinations you can teach. Be guided by your own child's words and interests in selecting sentences for the teaching sessions. If you use words that are familiar to your child, they will be easier to combine into two-word sentences, and the sessions will be more meaningful.

Although the focus of the sessions is now on teaching two-word sentences, you should continue to teach new single words. It is important to continue expanding your child's vocabulary. As in the past, be sure that you have planned the words and word combinations that you want to teach before starting the session. The teaching sessions are more likely to run smoothly if you are well organized and know exactly what you want your child to do.

Finally, we have said repeatedly that consistency is an essential part of this productive language program. Consistency is important not only during the 12-minute teaching sessions, but during the rest of the day as well. Not only is consistency required on the part of the "teacher," but also on the part of all family members who interact with the child. Each time someone gives a child who points or gestures a drink, it prolongs the difficulty for the child to learn the new contingencies or rules, namely, that the child must say a word to get what he or she wants. The person who asks your child to say a word should be prepared to wait until the word (or word approximation) is produced. If the word is not spoken, it is necessary to withhold the object that your child is seeking even if an outburst of temper occurs. Your child's compliance and success should be expected, but if resistance and protest occur, your child must not be rewarded. Obviously, requests for talking should not be made when these rules cannot be followed. If you are in a hurry to leave the house, if you are in the presence of friends or relatives who would weaken your capacity to withstand an outburst of temper, or if you are in a public place such as a restaurant where you are not able to control the situation, you should not demand speech. In other words, be careful to pick a time and place that will allow you to be consistent in your efforts to encourage your child to use speech. The capacity to choose the time and place to encourage talking is a major advantage that you as a parent have in this process, and it is wise to make a selection that offers the best chance for success.

STYLES OF INTERACTION TO ENCOURAGE TALKING

Once your child has learned to say two-word sentences easily in the teaching sessions, you can begin to generalize the use of sentences to other times during the day. By now you should be highly attentive to your child's attempts to say words. Many parents have said to us, "I never realized how many words my child can say."

One benefit of the teaching sessions is that parents develop the habit of attending to their child's speech, of constantly "listening with one ear." Their increased sensitivity to their child's attempts to speak yields more frequent opportunities for them to respond with praise and other rewards during the course of the day. The three strategies discussed in this section reflect styles of interaction that will encourage your child's speech if incorporated into your daily routine. The same styles of interaction discussed in Chapter 5 can be used here to stimulate the production of sentences outside of the teaching sessions. These techniques include asking questions, setting real-world contingencies, and providing informal language stimulation.

Asking Questions

Questions can be used to stimulate talking both within and outside of the teaching sessions. When asking a question, encourage your child to answer with a two-word sentence rather than a single word. For example, Nicole's mother was asking her to name objects in the bathroom:

Mother: (Pointing to Nicole's toothbrush.) "What's this?"
Nicole: "Toothbrush."
Mother: "That's right. It's a toothbrush. It's Nicole's toothbrush. Can you say Nicole's toothbrush?"

Nicole: "Cole toothbrush."
Mother: "Good girl. You said Nicole's toothbrush. What's this?"
Nicole: "Cole toothbrush."
Mother: "Good girl. Do you want to brush your teeth?"
Nicole: "Brush."
Mother: "Say, brush teeth."
Nicole: "Brush teeth."
Mother: "Good Nicole. What do you want to do?"
Nicole: "Brush teeth."
Mother: "What a smart girl." (Gives Nicole the toothbrush with a small amount of toothpaste as a reward because Nicole likes to brush her teeth.)

Nicole's mother turned a naturally rewarding situation to her advantage. She elicited appropriate two-word sentences in a situation in which Nicole usually did not talk. Not only that, but Nicole's mother did not rest with simple imitative responses. Instead, she immediately asked follow-up questions to elicit spontaneous two-word answers. This is an excellent technique that should be used often.

Setting Real-World Contingencies

Real-World contingencies can be used to make specific requests, which can be followed up with natural rewards, for talking outside of the teaching sessions. Select five or six situations in the course of a normal day where your child can be encouraged to use the sentences that have been learned. For example:

1. If your child wants more juice to drink require him or her to say *more juice* before filling the glass.
2. If your child wants to go outside to play, require him or her to say *go out* or *out please* before being permitted to leave the house.
3. Ask your child to say, for example, *Jeffrey up* or *up please* before picking him up or lifting him onto your lap.

Follow the same rules in these real-life situations that you follow in the teaching sessions. Tell your child clearly what you want him or her to say and then wait for an acceptable response before giving the desired object or outcome. Do not give in once you have made a request for speech. It is also important for other members of the family to follow these same rules. Failure to be consistent will prolong the task and make it more difficult for your child to learn to use two-word sentences.

To help your child succeed, make sure he or she has some practice saying the sentences you request. Practice the sentence in the language session before asking your child to say it at other times during the day. Also, make sure you have the time to follow through with your request. For example, do not ask your child to say *more juice* if you are in a hurry to eat dinner and cannot wait calmly for him or her to answer.

Requesting speech outside the sessions is one of the most effective ways to help your child use speech naturally to communicate with others. Ask your child to talk as frequently as possible. The more he or she talks outside the sessions, the faster language learning will progress.

Providing Informal Language Stimulation

The informal language stimulation suggestions given in Chapter 5 can be used to encourage two-word sentences also. Speak to your child as much as possible outside the teaching sessions and be sure to reward his or her attempts to communicate with you. Talk to your child about what you are doing and listen carefully when he or she speaks. If your child is trying to tell you something, but does not use the right words, suggest words and help your child say them. If your child responds to your speech with a single-word comment such as *brush,* suggest an appropriate two-word sentence such as *mommy's brush.* Expose your child to language as often as possible. Try to make his or her attempts at communication simple and provide naturally occurring rewards and ample praise. These are important ways to help your child learn to talk and achieve independent verbal communication.

EVENTS AND PROPS TO ENCOURAGE TALKING

The final section suggests events and props that can be used to teach two-word sentences during the language sessions. It also lists ways to encourage the use of two-word sentences outside the teaching sessions. Many teaching suggestions are given in this section, so you may find this part of the manual useful as a reference. It may be helpful to look through it when you are deciding how to teach different kinds of sentences to your child. Usually, only one of the events presented in this section is needed in a teaching session. The same event can be used for 2 or 3 days in a row. It is time to switch to a new event or prop when your child begins to give signs of boredom with the old one. It is also appropriate to change when your child has learned the sentences you are teaching and is ready to practice talking about new things.

In general, these are age-appropriate pretend activities that most children who are ready to begin saying two- (and three-) word sentences will find interesting. These pretend activities and events not only stimulate talking, but they help children understand the meanings of the sentences they are learning to say. For example, actions such as *doll jumping, dog swimming,* or *car rolling,* which would be difficult to describe otherwise, can be demonstrated and made meaningful. You can use an entire event or any part of the activity in a single teaching session. Although the emphasis in this chapter is on teaching two-word sentences, you should continue to teach new single words during the sessions as well, particularly the action verbs and concepts that may arise during the play activities.

Games to Play

Bathing a Doll

Objects needed are a doll with clothes, a sponge, and a towel. Begin by undressing the doll and asking your child to say the following sentences as you remove items of clothing:

baby's shoe	baby's hat
shoe off	hat off
baby's sock	baby's dress
sock off	dress off
baby's pants	
pants off	

Then wash the doll with the sponge, and teach your child to say:

baby's hair	baby's ears	baby's feet
wash hair	wash ears	wash feet
baby's eyes	baby's mouth	baby's tummy
wash eyes	wash mouth	wash tummy
baby's nose	baby's neck	baby's hands
wash nose	wash neck	wash hands

mommy's washing or (child's name) washing

Dry the doll and teach *wipe hair, wipe eyes, mommy's wiping,* and numerous other combinations. Similarly, dress the doll and teach *pants on, dress on, sock on,* and other simple combinations. Other sentences that can be taught while dressing and undressing the doll are: *push up, pull down, tie hat,* and *all done.*

Tea Party

Good objects to use to create a pretend tea party include a doll, cups, plates, teapot, spoons, and cookies. Begin by setting the table for yourself, your child, and the doll (baby). As you put each item on the table, teach:

baby's cup	baby's spoon
cup down	spoon down
baby's plate	mommy's cup
plate down	mommy's plate
baby's cookie	daddy's spoon
cookie down	daddy's cookie

Then put the top on the teapot, pour tea for everyone, stir the tea, drink it, and eat the cookies. Sentences to teach as you perform these actions include:

top on	mommy's tea	eat cookie
pour tea	mommy's drinking	mommy's cookie
stir tea	baby's tea	mommy's eating
drink tea	baby's drinking	baby's cookie

Serve more tea and cookies to everyone and then clean up the tea party. Sentences to teach include:

more tea	wipe spoon	all gone
more cookie	wipe mouth	wash spoon
tea please	wipe baby	wash pot
cookie please	wipe cup	wash cup
wipe plate	wipe pot	wash plate

Putting a Doll to Bed

Props needed are a doll with clothes, a bed, pillow, blanket, and toothbrush. Begin by brushing the doll's teeth and undressing the doll. Then put the pillow on the bed, put the doll in the bed, cover it with a blanket, and say good night. Sentences to teach are:

baby's teeth	baby's shoes	pillow here
brush teeth	shoes off	baby's bed
baby's toothbrush	baby's socks	baby's blanket
baby's pants	socks off	blanket up
pants off	baby's dress	baby's sleeping
light off	dress off	night-night baby.

Baking Cookies with Play-Doh

Good objects for creating a baking scene are Play-Doh, a cookie sheet, animal-shaped cookie cutters, a rolling pin, and a box for an oven. Begin by kneading the dough and rolling it out flat. Cut out cookies with the cookie cutters and put them on the cookie sheet. Put the cookies in the oven to bake and pretend to eat them when they are done. Of course, you should caution your child that the cookies are not real. Wash and dry the dishes when you are finished. Sentences to teach are:

squeeze dough	bake cookies	eat kitty
roll dough	all done	eat bear
push down	doggy eat	wipe mouth
cut dough	doggy down (as you	mommy's eating
cut dog	place doggy on	mommy's washing
cut kitty	cookie sheet)	wash pan
cut bear	kitty down	wipe pan
	bear down	

Playing "Simon Says"

Play this game by putting your hands above your head and saying *hands up*. Ask your child to perform the same actions and to repeat what you say. Use as many different actions as your child can imitate and describe. Some actions to use include:

hands up	clap hands
hands down	touch head
foot up	touch nose
foot down	touch mouth
stand up	wave hands
sit down	stamp feet
lay down	fall down
jump up	jump down

Making Puzzles

Ask your child to repeat two-word sentences as you do a puzzle together. For example, if you are working on a simple four-piece puzzle containing a boot, a hat, a coat, and an umbrella, you can teach the following sentences and more:

boot out	boot please	coat please
coat out	push boot	push coat
hat out	turn boot	turn coat
umbrella out	boot in	coat in
dump pieces	all done	hat in

Looking at Books

Books are always good to use in the teaching sessions. Describe the pictures in the books with appropriate two-word sentences and ask your child to repeat what you say. *Do not read the stories to your child* when you are teaching words. Of course, listening to stories can be a source of enjoyment, but if your child is just sitting and listening, he or she is not actively participating in your efforts to produce talking. In order to learn to use speech, your child must take an active part in the process; he or she must name and describe objects and events at this point in development. In addition, children who are just beginning to speak often do not understand written language, even the form of written language used in the simplest books. Therefore, talk about the pictures. Use simple sentences that you want your child to learn to say. Remember to ask your child questions about these events. For example, if you are describing the Jack and Jill rhyme, you may suggest the following sentences:

boy running	girl falling	Jill down
boy falling	water spilling	Jack down
girl running	pail falling	carry water

Telephone Games

Use a toy telephone to practice saying hello and goodbye. Pretend to call someone your child knows well, like a grandparent, brother, or sister. Dial the phone, help your child to hold the receiver to his or her ear, and then say *hello* and *goodbye*. Hang up the receiver and start again with another call. Sentences to teach are:

call grandma	hi grandma	bye grandpa
call grandpa	hi grandpa	phone up
dial phone	bye grandma	phone down

Generalization Outside the Sessions

The following situations illustrate ways to encourage your child to use two-word sentences to describe events that occur during the course of an average day. It is best to practice new two-word sentences during the 12-

minute language training sessions before encouraging them outside the sessions.

Take time during the day to talk about what you and your child are doing. Describe your own actions using two-word sentences and ask your child to repeat them. Good activities to describe are bathing, washing hands and face before and after meals, dressing and undressing, setting the table, cooking and eating meals, washing dishes and clothes, cleaning house, and riding in a car. If your child enjoys these activities, be sure that he or she talks about them before being allowed to engage in them.

1. Sing songs with your child that include short, repetitive phrases. Examples of children's songs are listed in Appendix B.
2. Require your child to say *coat on, hat on, socks on,* and so forth before being allowed to put them on to go outside.
3. Require your child to say *TV on* or *TV please* before turning the television on.
4. Require your child to say *light on* or *light off* before being allowed to flick the light switch.
5. Require your child to say *more* or *please* with the appropriate food name before giving a snack or treat.
6. Require your child to say *up please* before picking him or her up or *down please* before putting him or her down.
7. Require your child to say *out please* before being allowed to go outside.
8. Require your child to say *hello* and *goodbye* to friends and neighbors who may come to the house each day. The letter carrier may be a good person to greet each day, for example.
9. When you take your child to the supermarket, encourage saying *hello* and *goodbye* to the cashier.
10. Give your child a chance to say *hi daddy* or *hi grandma* when they call on the telephone.
11. Practice labeling parts of your own body, your child's, and other members of your family at other times during the day. For example, have your child name his or her own body parts while taking a bath, washing up before and after meals, and dressing.
12. Practice labeling items of clothing while dressing and undressing your child, folding laundry, and/or looking through a clothes closet.
13. Take a walk around the house and label objects. For example:

mommy's bed	(child's name) bed	daddy's chair
mommy's light	(child's name) light	daddy's book

14. Take a walk outside the house and describe what you see. For example:

daddy's car	big tree	mommy's car
doggie's dish	small bug	ride car

7

Teaching Complex Sentences

GOALS, PREREQUISITES, AND A WORD OF CAUTION

The final goal of the language program is to teach your child to use complex sentences that are at least three words in length. As was the case with single words and two-word sentences, the first step is to encourage your child to say these longer sentences during a formal teaching session and then to use them at other times during the day. Before beginning this part of the program, your child should be producing two-word sentences easily within the teaching sessions and with increasing frequency during spontaneous comments throughout the day. If your child has not reached this level of productive language development, you should continue to teach two-word sentences and to expand his or her single-word vocabulary. Three- and four-word sentences should only be taught if two-word sentences are mastered. There is little to be gained from pushing too far beyond your child's current ability. On the contrary, your current success may be disrupted by demanding longer and more complex sentences than your child is able to produce at this time.

If your child is ready to begin producing three-word sentences, then there is no doubt that your achievements to date should be applauded. Not only is your child about to enter a new phase of development, but he or she is better equipped to handle this new phase. First, the shift from two-word combinations to longer sentences is usually an easier task than learning to say single words or combining single words into two-word productions. As we mentioned earlier, the beginning phases of this program are the most difficult. By this phase, children are more compliant, have acquired reasonably large productive vocabularies, are more likely to use words rather than gestures to communicate, and have learned to combine single words into short phrases. Second, and of equal importance, at this level of development children have begun to experience the sense of competence and satisfaction that accompanies successful communication through talking. Increasingly, this sense of satisfaction will become the primary motivation for talking and will gradually replace the need for other rewards such as edibles or special treats, the contingent administration of objects that are requested, and constant praise.

However, do not become overconfident or ease up with your efforts at this point. It is at this phase in the language program that parents, pleased with their child's progress to date, are tempted to relax their teaching efforts. You should be cautioned not to abandon the formal teaching sessions or relax your efforts too greatly at this time. The problem is that your child's ability to say words and to communicate by using speech is still a newly learned skill; it is not an automatic or well-established pattern yet. As such, it requires additional practice and reward to insure that it will be retained and become a firm part of your child's everyday behavior. Nevertheless, your child's success up to this point should be a rewarding experience for you. Revel in it because you have earned this satisfaction, but be aware that the job is not over. The important task of acquiring three- and four-word sentences lies ahead, but the light is visible at the end of the tunnel. We are nearing the point where your child's use of talking for communication is virtually irreversible. This fact should give you the incentive and strength to push on with vigor.

THE USE OF COMPLEX SENTENCES

This portion of the language program is concerned with teaching children to say sentences that are beginning to sound adultlike. The easiest way to start is to teach children to expand the two-word phrases that they already know in order to produce longer sentences. Do not introduce new words for this task. Your child's efforts should be focused on stringing together familiar words into three-word sentences. The illustration that follows shows how to help your child combine the two-word sentences he or she already knows to form longer, complex sentences. In addition, ideas for sentences to teach and several different teaching activities are described at the end of this chapter.

An Illustration

Brian and his mother are in the middle of their regular morning teaching session. Brian's mother began the session by practicing single words and two-word sentences that were familiar to Brian. Now she is trying to teach him to combine familiar two-word sentences into new three-word sentences. Brian can say *baby drink* and *drink milk*. His mother is teaching him to combine these sentences to say *baby drinks milk*.

Mother: (Using a doll and toy bottle as props, she pretends to feed the doll with the bottle while saying, "The baby drinks milk." Then she asks Brian to imitate.) "Brian, say baby drinks milk."
Brian: "Dwink milk." (Not rewarded.)
Mother: "*Baby* drinks milk."
Brian: "Baby dwink."
Mother: "Good. You said baby drinks." (She gives Brian a piece of apple as a reward.)

Brian had trouble saying three words together, so his mother tried a different strategy. She used a technique that had worked before when she was teaching Brian to put two words together into one sentence. She prompted Brian to say the two sentences separately, one right after the other. Then she prompted him to say the sentences closer and closer in time until he could say the three words together clearly.

Mother: "Baby drinks. Brian, say baby drinks."
Brian: "Baby dwink."
Mother: "Good boy. Brian, say drinks milk."
Brian: "Dwink milk."
Mother: "Good, Brian. Say baby drinks."
Brian: "Baby dwink."
Mother: "Drinks milk."
Brian: "Dwink milk."
Mother: "Baby drinks."
Brian: "Baby dwink."
Mother: "Drinks milk."
Brian: "Dwink milk."
Mother: "Baby drinks milk."
Brian: "Baby dwink milk."
Mother: "Good boy. You said baby drinks milk." (Gives him a piece of apple.) "Baby drinks milk."
Brian: "Baby dwink milk."
Mother: "Good boy. You said baby drinks milk." (She smiles and gives him another piece of apple.)

Brian's mother rehearsed *baby drinks milk* five more times to give Brian practice saying the three-word sentence clearly. She then taught him two other three-word sentences (*baby drinks juice, mommy drinks juice*) and ended the session by rehearsing single words and two-word sentences.

The technique used by Brian's mother to help him say three words together is one that has been described in earlier chapters. The three-word sentence, *baby drinks milk,* is broken down into its smaller, two-word parts—*baby drinks* and *drinks milk.* These smaller parts are first imitated separately and then closer and closer together in time until a request to say the three words together can be completed successfully. The three-word sentence is then practiced several times before other new sentences are taught. Breaking down longer sentences into shorter parts before requesting imitation of the whole sentence is a good way to help a child learn to string words together.

Another point to note from Brian's teaching session is that he had difficulty pronouncing the word *drink*. Children often have trouble saying certain sounds, and like Brian, they may say *dwink* for *drink* or *twain* for *train*. These kinds of "mistakes," often referred to as "baby talk," are common in the speech of young children, and they tend to disappear as children grow older and have more practice speaking. Do not be concerned with these misarticulations at this stage of your child's language development.

As we said earlier, children may also make mistakes speaking because they do not understand all the grammar rules of their language. For example, Brian said *baby drink* instead of *baby drinks* because he did not yet understand that verbs in these kinds of sentences always end in *s*. Mistakes in grammar, like baby-talk mistakes, should not concern you at this stage of your child's language development. Children will learn basic grammar rules without direct instruction as long as they are exposed to people who speak correctly. It appears that if you speak correctly to your child, you will not have to make a special effort to teach basic grammar rules. Your child will begin to imitate your correct speech when he or she is able to understand its importance.

The language sessions may become less structured as your child speaks more readily and produces more complex sentences. Essentially, the sessions may become play periods that focus on talking. Do not underestimate the benefit of these less formal interactions. For one thing, they provide the consistency (12 minutes per day for at least 5 days per week) that is essential for the success of this program. For another, they give an opportunity for prolonged verbal interaction that allows for the rehearsal of existing language and the expansion to new words and sentences. However, it will continue to be important to reward your child for the words that he or she produces during the sessions.

In addition, it continues to be desirable to require your child to speak at other times during the day. The naturally occurring rewards will help motivate your child to learn to say new words and sentences and to continue using the language that he or she already knows. Continue to talk to your child about what you are doing and encourage your child to speak to you. An important change is to ask questions that require two- and three-word answers, rather than single-word utterances or simple yes–no responses. Remember that asking questions is an excellent way to promote talking. For example, if you are baking a cake with your child, ask:

> "What are you doing?"
> "Where's the butter?"
> "Whose bowl is this?"
> "What do you want?"

If your child does not answer correctly, gives only a partially correct response, or gives a one-word answer, provide the appropriate answers and ask your child to repeat them. Then, ask your question again to give more practice. For example:

Mother: "Where's the butter?"
Chris: "Table."
Mother: "It's on the table. Say on the table."
Chris: "On the table."
Mother: "Good boy. On the table, Where's the butter, Chris?"
Chris: "On the table."
Mother: "That's right. On the table."

The more you talk to your child outside the sessions and encourage him or her to talk to you, the faster your child's speech is likely to progress. Fortunately, this need will not continue indefinitely; you are approaching the end point. For now, do your best to fill your child's world with language and provide the necessary help to make his or her attempts successful and rewarding.

THE DELETION OF EDIBLE REWARDS

At the beginning of this manual, we said that contingent food rewards, objects, and praise were only temporary strategies for getting children to begin talking. Ultimately, talking will bring its own rewards, and food, objects, and praise will no longer be needed. Children who are able to talk easily are rewarded naturally. They are no longer limited to using vague gestures and can ask directly for food, toys, or whatever they may want. We have suggested that from a child's perspective, the ability to communicate one's thoughts by talking is almost magical. A child learns that thoughts can be translated into language, which others understand and respond to readily. In addition, talking makes it easier to interact socially with adults. Children no longer have to run to adults to gain their attention. They can simply talk to them from across the room. In other words, the rewards that sustain language eventually come naturally in the act of communication of one's thoughts and needs.

When behaviors such as talking are new they should be rewarded every time that they occur in order to produce a maximum effect. This is called *continuous reward*. When talking is well-learned, it should be rewarded less, that is only some of the time, in order to achieve a maximum effect. We have referred to this as *partial reward*. This result in which more talking occurs with fewer edibles and less praise is a paradoxical, but lawful principle of behavior. It is appropriate now to provide partial rewards for talking. This strategy will accomplish two things: (1) the gradual elimination of edibles and praise as rewards including the M & M's, chocolate chips, and raisins that were encouraged in the beginning; and (2) the strengthening of your child's tendency to talk. Once your child is using three and four word sentences readily, it is appropriate for you to allow the naturally occurring consequences of speech to serve as the primary rewards for talking. Thus, as we promised in the beginning, the use of edible rewards should be terminated at that point.

Although food rewards and constant praise are no longer necessary to maintain productive language, it is still important for parents to encourage their children's speech and provide regular opportunities for practice. Thus, as parents, you should try to encourage speech as much as possible at any time of day. It is also, important to be aware of ways that you might inadvertently discourage your child's talking. Avoid comments like, "Don't bother me now!" or "For heaven's sake, stop that chattering!" for they may effectively and unintentionally discourage speech if repeated often enough. It is difficult for parents to be attentive constantly and to "hang on" to their child's every word; fortunately, this is not necessary. A positive attitude toward speech production is important, however. As parents, you have worked hard to help your child learn to speak. Allow yourself to share your pleasure with your child for these day-to-day accomplishments, and it will help to keep language learning a positive experience.

SOCIAL FACTORS: GENERALIZATION
TO NEW SITUATIONS AND OTHER ADULTS

It should be kept in mind that it is common for 2- and 3-year-old children to manifest some degree of anxiety when they are in strange situations or in the company of unfamiliar adults. Children's behaviors often appear less mature, shy, and inhibited in strange situations. They are less willing to leave the security of their parents to join in the activities that are taking place. In the case of the language-delayed child, initially unfamiliar situations often are a cause of disappointment to the parent. When there is clear progress during the speech training sessions and frequent use of spontaneous speech within the familiar setting of the home, it is both surprising and discouraging when your child "refuses" to talk to unfamiliar friends or relatives. Rest assured that it is common for the child who is beginning to speak in two- and three-word phrases within the home to display little of this recently acquired ability when in the company of strangers or in unfamiliar situations.

Children, like adults, find it easier to speak when among close friends and within familiar surroundings. The young child who has only recently acquired the capacity to communicate through the use of words may experience anxiety when called upon to perform in an unfamiliar setting. It is wise to anticipate a period of transition during which your child's productive language in unfamiliar social situations is less mature than when talking in the security of his or her own home. You must expect that, for a time, your child's speech with you at home will be more mature and spontaneous than in your neighbor's kitchen, at the local playgroup, or when your mother-in-law visits.

Once children begin to speak using three-and four-word sentences, it is important to actively encourage them to speak to other adults. Keep in mind that speech-delayed children usually do not have much experience talking to people other than their teacher—often their mother. It is only natural to expect shyness with other adults at first; this is a natural event in development. For the speech-delayed child, it appears essential to encourage the generalization of talking to other adults in a systematic way. By doing so, this phase of your child's language development, an important goal of this program, will be accomplished efficiently.

There are several ways to encourage talking in unfamiliar social situations. You can make an effort to include your child in conversations that occur when you are outside your home or with different adults. Once your child reaches the level of three- and four-word sentences, try to encour-

age talking with the grocer, a salesclerk, or a neighbor whenever possible. Preschool can also provide an opportunity for your child to practice speaking to another adult. Most preschool teachers are willing to be firm but supportive with children who need to be encouraged to speak, and many would be delighted to assist with this valuable function, if requested to do so by parents.

It is reasonable to encourage your child to use the words and sentences that he or she is saying spontaneously within the home, but it is inappropriate to insist that your child use this same level of productive language outside of the home initially. Children who are new at talking, particularly speech-delayed children, need practice talking to other adults in other settings. As children gain practice talking with other adults, their inhibition in the presence of strangers and strange situations will lessen, particularly if rewards are presented contingently in these new social settings. Thus, you may be temporarily denied the pleasure of demonstrating your child's recent accomplishments in unfamiliar situations despite the knowledge that they are performed successfully in your home. However, if you specifically encourage your child to speak in new situations, this problem can be overcome.

Answering Questions for Other Adults

Once a child is speaking four-and five-word sentences to other adults, the goals of this training program are nearly complete. But there is one additional area where difficulties may arise as a result of a child's earlier productive-language delay. We have said that children who are slow to talk are often shy in new social situations and that these children should practice speaking to adults other than their parents. When children begin to speak to other adults, it may appear that their inhibition has disappeared. However, on a number of occasions, we have found that the shyness is elicited primarily when the child is called upon to answer specific questions by an unfamiliar adult. For example, a child may readily initiate a conversation with his grandfather, whom he sees about once every 2 months, but may become quiet and inhibited if grandfather asks what he got for his birthday. The child may not respond verbally and may even drift away from the situation. This form of inhibition is more subtle than an outright refusal to talk with other adults and may be overlooked more easily. It is useful to watch your child's performance when another adult asks a series of questions about an event that may have occurred or about his or her mother or sister. If your child displays inhibition in social situations, it may be useful to begin a trial period of training to reduce this inhibition. You can begin to practice reciting well-learned information (the alphabet or a song, for example) in social situations with your child so that he or she may become more comfortable talking under these relatively new and demanding social situations.

A second reason for encouraging the recitation of information is more cognitive than social. The child who is slow to speak often has missed many opportunities to perform in elaborate question-and-answer situations, even those who have experienced the question-and-answer sessions suggested in Chapters 5 and 6. Remember, it is more difficult to retrieve information from one's memory than it is simply to imitate what another person says. Similarly, it appears easier to retrieve information that you wish to speak about than to remember details about questions that another person asks. That is to say, it appears easier for children to speak spontaneously about events in their world than to answer highly specific questions that they may not remember easily, particularly if the children are anxious. For example, your child may find it easy to speak in four- and five-word sentences but may experience difficulty when asked, "What did you do at Johnny's house today?" Speech-delayed children may not have had much experience retrieving and answering questions that they are not thinking about at that moment and may not know what to say. The same children may be able to respond correctly if the question is more specific and if more cues are provided. For example, if asked, "What did you watch on TV at Johnny's house today?" a child may quickly respond with "Sesame Street."

The combination of inexperience with remembering and reporting information and shyness in some social situations may combine to create an impression that your child is cognitively and socially immature. This seemingly innocuous combination of inexperience and shyness can have serious implications for the impression your child may convey to other people. As children approach 3 years of age and older, our society places an increasingly heavier reliance on productive language to evaluate children in both informal and formal settings. Preschool teachers make judgments about children's cognitive and social maturity based, in large part, on verbal responsiveness to questions. At younger ages, in particular, a teacher's impression is formed through interaction with the child in the classroom and through the child's interactions with other children. Formal developmental evaluations performed by psychologists require productive language in response to questions. Conventional testing instruments such as the Stanford–Binet Scale of Intelligence and the McCarthy Scales for Children rely heavily on verbal responses to the examiner, who is an unfamiliar person. It is important for parents to know that conventional psychological testing with preschool children requires the ability to remember and recite information to unfamiliar adults under mildly threatening circumstances. Thus, these suggested exercises are important because they may prepare your child to handle these potentially threatening social-cognitive situations.

There are steps that parents can take to provide children with the experiences needed in these formal and informal evaluation situations. The 12-minute teaching sessions can be used to practice more sophisticated cognitive tasks than those suggested up to this point. These could include reciting the alphabet, learning the numbers from 1 to 20, and singing some of the songs that are included in Appendix B. There should be two steps in the process of instruction. First, the 12-minute sessions can be used to acquire the information under comfortable circumstances involving the child and his or her primary teacher, usually the mother. The daily teaching sessions can be used to teach one of the tasks, such as reciting the alphabet, until the child is able to repeat the entire alphabet on request. The second step is for the teacher and child to repeat their routine in the presence of another adult. Initially, it may be necessary for you to prompt your child in the presence of another adult, but soon it will not be necessary. Both you and your friend should reward the child with praise and attention upon successful completion of the task. As your child becomes more confident and competent in the presence of another adult, the group might be made larger. For example, your child could be asked to show grandmother and grandfather how well he or she can recite the alphabet. Your contingent praise and attention and the praise of other adults will help reduce your child's inhibition to speak in less familiar social situations. This same procedure can be repeated with counting and with singing songs. In each case, it is important to be sure that your child has learned the information and can repeat it in your presence before being asked to display this skill in the presence of other individuals.

It appears that at this point in your child's development, retrieving and reciting information in social situations may be improved in a relatively short time, perhaps as little as 3 or 4 weeks. However, it may be best to allow 2 months, because it is worth insuring that your child has attained this important skill.

CONCLUDING COMMENTS

This final chapter on teaching complex sentences has been relatively brief. The techniques and procedures described in earlier sections are now familiar to you and can be used to help your child acquire a more complex level of productive language. Your child has progressed dramatically up to this point. The reliance on gestures and the tendency to resist requests for speech have been replaced by the ability to use spoken words for communication with others. The success you have had in assisting your child in the development of multiple word sentences is proof in itself that he or she is far more cooperative and less resistant than ever before. This reduction in resistant and noncompliant behavior has been a central goal of this program. Moreover, the procedures to assist with further changes are essentially the same as those described in earlier chapters. In a sense, the brevity of this chapter is a result of what has been accomplished already.

It is important to recognize that the shift from one- and two-word utterances to three-, four- and five-word complex sentences represents a major advance in your child's language development. This shift marks the end of the long and deliberate acquisition of single words needed to provide the foundation for the production of two-word combinations. The transition to three-word sentences marks the beginning of a period of increasingly rapid progress in language production. It has been our experience and the experience of others that once a child is using three-word sentences, longer sentences are highly likely to come spontaneously. It is as though the achievement of three-word sentences places the previously delayed child back on the course of natural language development. Prompting and rewards for talking become much less important. Further language development occurs almost automatically. The previously language-delayed child may continue to benefit from praise and perhaps even occasional rewards for the use of four- and five-word sentences. Nevertheless, rewards are more likely to occur in response to naturally occurring events of the day, including conversations between your child and you and between your child and his or her peers. It is during this period of rapid expansion in sentence length and complexity that the stimulation of productive language comes more from the "language environment" than from formal teaching sessions or from the contingent use of edible rewards or other consequences.

By now, not only should you be aware of your child's speech, but also of the degree to which your comments, including conversations with your child, serve to make possible the emergence of complex language. Your efforts as a teacher have made it possible for your child to become a partner in conversations with others. A remaining task is to remember that the communicative partnership requires the continuing participation of both parties. Do not hesitate to speak to your child when an occasion presents itself; verbal communication with your child is an important vehicle for continued cognitive, social, and emotional growth from the preschool period on through adolescence.

EVENTS AND PROPS TO ENCOURAGE TALKING

At the end of Chapter 6, we suggested several events and props that could be used to teach two-word sentences. Several examples of specific two-word sentences were also provided. In this section, examples showing how these same events and props can be used to promote three-word sentences are given. As noted before, usually only one of these events will be needed in a single teaching session. Switch to a new event if your child seems bored or has learned the sentences you are teaching and is ready to practice talking about new things. In general, these are age-

appropriate pretend activities that most children who are ready to use three-word sentences find interesting. Remember that although the emphasis here is on teaching three-word sentences, you should continue to teach new single words and two-word sentences during the sessions as well. You should also include your child's name with each of the sentences to be learned.

Games to Play

Bathing a Doll

Objects needed are a doll with clothes, a sponge, and a towel. Begin by undressing the doll and asking your child to say the following sentences as you remove items of clothing.

baby's shoe off
baby's sock off
baby's hat off
baby's dress off
baby's pants off

As you wash the doll with a sponge, teach the following:

wash baby's hair	wash baby's neck
wash baby's eyes	wash baby's feet
wash baby's nose	wash baby's tummy
wash baby's ears	wash baby's hands
wash baby's mouth	

Dry the doll and teach: *wipe baby's hair, wipe baby's eyes, mom's wiping hair,* and so forth. Similarly, dress the doll and teach: *baby's pants on, baby's dress on, baby's sock on,* and other three-word combinations.

Tea Party

Objects needed are a doll, cups, plates, spoons, a teapot, and cookies. Begin by setting the table for yourself, your child, and the doll (baby). Teach the following:

baby's cup down	baby's cookie down
baby's plate down	mommy's cup down
baby's spoon down	mommy's plate down

Then put the top on the teapot, pour tea for everyone, stir the tea, drink it, and eat the cookies. Sentences to teach include:

put the top on   mommy's drinking tea
pour mommy's tea   baby's drinking tea
pour baby's tea   eat mommy's cookie
stir mommy's tea   eat baby's cookie
stir baby's tea

Give more tea and cookies to everyone and then clean up the tea party. Teach the following:

more tea please   wash baby's plate
more cookies please   wipe mommy's cup
no more tea   wipe baby's plate
tea's all gone   wipe mommy's mouth
wash mommy's cup   wipe baby's mouth

Putting a Doll to Bed

Props needed are a doll with clothes, a bed, pillow, blanket, and toothbrush. Begin by brushing the doll's teeth and undressing the doll. Then put the pillow on the bed, put the doll into the bed, and cover it with a blanket. Sentences to teach include:

brush baby's teeth   climb into bed
baby's shoes off   pull blanket up
baby's socks off   head on pillow
baby's dress off   go to sleep
baby's pants off   good night baby

Playing Simon Says

This game is also fun when other members of the family play along. Some commands to teach are:

mommy, hands down   mommy, clap hands
mommy, foot up   mommy, touch head
daddy, foot down   daddy, touch nose
mommy, stand up   mommy, wave hands
mommy, sit down   mommy, stamp foot
daddy, lie down   daddy, fall down
daddy, jump down   daddy, roll over
mommy, jump up   mommy, bend down

Appendix A

ARTICULATION PROBLEMS

When children first learn to speak, they often fail to say words clearly or distinctly. They omit or add sounds to words and tend to slur certain sounds together. Speaking is, in part, a highly skilled motor action, and some articulation problems may arise because in the beginning the necessary motor skills may not be well coordinated. Children have varying degrees of difficulty coordinating their lips and tongue, breathing and forming the shape of their mouth when trying to speak. They must learn to control their breathing and the flow of air past the vocal cords in order to produce the right combination of sounds as well as the pattern of inflection and intonation that characterizes the particular spoken language that they are learning. These problems are common to virtually *all* children as they learn to speak, are part of a natural process, and should not be a major concern during the early stages of a child's speech development

Certain sounds are easier to produce and appear early in children's speech. Others are more difficult and some combinations and blends may not be mastered until the second or third grade. Appendix A.1 contains an overall timetable of the age at which most children can pronounce certain sounds at the beginning, middle, and end of words. Keep in mind that children vary greatly in their speech and language development. Some 3-year-olds can say ca*k*e, *t*able, be*d,* wagon, and hou*s*e. Those who cannot usually learn to do so with practice. What you should realize is that some words like *sp*oon and *tr*ain that seem easy to you contain more difficult sounds that may not appear in your child's speech until the sixth or seventh year.

With the aid of the teaching techniques described in this appendix and with much practice speaking, most of these articulation problems will diminish—even disappear.

Appendix A.1:
An Articulation Timetable
Sample Words

Age	Sound	Beginning	Middle	End
3	m	*m*onkey	ham*m*er	comb
	p	*p*ipe	ap*p*le	ca*p*
	b	*b*ook	ba*b*y	tu*b*
4	k	*c*at	cra*ck*ers	ca*ke*
	g	*g*un	wa*g*on	e*gg*
	f	*f*ork	ele*ph*ant	kni*f*e
5	d	*d*og	lad*d*er	be*d*
	t	*t*able	po*t*ato	ha*t*
6	r	*r*adio	ca*rr*ot	ca*r*
	l	*l*amp	gal*l*on	be*ll*
	sh	*sh*oe	gas sta*t*ion	fi*sh*
	ch	*ch*air	mat*ch*es	sandwi*ch*
7	v	*v*acuum	tele*v*ision	sto*v*e
	th	*th*umb	too*th*brush	tee*th*
	s	*s*aw	pen*c*il	hou*se*
	z	*z*ipper	sci*ss*ors	key*s*
7	blends	*sp*oon	*sk*ate	*st*ars
		*fl*ag	*cl*ock	*bl*ocks
		*cr*ayons	*tr*ain	*br*ush

However, some children have special articulation problems that may require professional attention. If a major articulation problem persists once your child is speaking in sentences, he or she should be seen by a physician for a medical examination, an audiologist for a hearing evaluation, and a certified speech therapist for a speech and language assessment. For example, on occasion children who have experienced recurrent ear infections are left with a collection of fluid in the middle ear which interferes with the transmission of sound. It may make it difficult for a child with fluid in the middle ear to hear certain frequencies and sound patterns clearly. Thus, if you have reason to believe that your child may not be hearing some of the words you are saying, professional advice should be sought before attempts to correct misarticulations are made.

GENERAL COMMENTS

If you are working on articulation problems during a language session, it is important to have your child look at your mouth as you say the words. Watching your mouth and lips move as you speak helps your child to imitate the different sounds you want him or her to say. To encourage improvement, reward only your child's best articulations; do not reward poor productions if your child can say the word more distinctly. The words you select for improvement should be those that are already familiar to your child. It is easier for your child to practice the correct pronunciation of words that he or she already knows, but mispronounces.

Although it is important to work on improving the articulation problems that we discuss here, it is also critical to recognize that certain misarticulations are a normal part of language development. Many children say *wun* for *run, pacake* for *pancake, andy* for *candy, no* for *nose, apa* for *apple*. For the most part, these misarticulations are relatively minor and generally do not prevent a child from being understood by others. They are the kinds of misarticulation that, in time, tend to disappear spontaneously. Even when major misarticulations cause your child to be misunderstood by others, if your child says only a few words, it is preferable to reward his or her attempts. Even misarticulated first words help your child to establish a firm disposition to use words. Your child should have a strong willingness to speak before a concentrated effort is made to improve pronunciation.

In the beginning, it is more important that your child uses speech rather than gestures alone; it is more important to develop a large vocabulary, even with misarticulated words, than to acquire only a few words that are correctly produced. In addition, it is more important that your child be praised for any attempted word that is recognizable rather than discouraged from saying anything except correctly articulated words. Once your child's tendency to speak is firmly established and two-word sentences are used, then it is time to help with pronunciation.

OMITTING SOUNDS

One of the most common problems children have when learning to say new words is the omission of certain sounds. For example; they say *up* for *cup* or *dow* for *down*. As they attempt longer words, they may have difficulty stringing together all of the component parts. There are several ways you can help your child overcome this common problem of omitting middle, initial, and final consonants of words.

Omitting Middle Consonants

Children sometimes fail to say the middle parts of words. For example; they may say pa–cake for *pancake* or *wa–er* for *water*. Words with more than one syllable can be separated into their component parts. You can ask a child to say each part separately, one right after the other. When the individual parts are successfully produced, bring the parts closer and closer together in time, and eventually ask the child to say the whole word. For example, in teaching the word *pancake,* ask your child to say *pan* then *cake* several times in a row before asking for the whole word, *pancake.* Let's look at an example of this teaching technique.

Robert usually says *pacake* for *pancake.* His mother begins by teaching Robert to say the words *pan* and *cake* separately.

Mother: "Pan, Robert. Say pan.,"
Robert: "Pa."
Mother: "Try again, Robert. Say pan."
Robert: "Pan."
Mother: "Good boy. You said pan." (Mother rewards Robert with praise and a piece of potato chip.)
Mother: "Now Robert, say cake."
Robert: "Cake."
Mother: "Good boy, Robert. You said cake." (Mother praises Robert again and gives him another piece of potato chip.)

Mother then proceeds to ask Robert to say the words *pan* and *cake* closer and closer together, finally asking him to say the whole word, *pancake.*

Mother: "Robert, say pan."
Robert: "Pan."
Mother: "Robert, say cake."
Robert: "Cake."
Mother: "Say pan."
Robert: "Pan."
Mother: "Say cake."
Robert: "Cake."
Mother: "Pan."
Robert: "Pan."
Mother: "Cake."
Robert: "Cake."
Mother: "Say pancake."
Robert: "Pancake."
Mother: "Good boy, Robert. You said pancake." (Mother smiles, gives him a hug, and a piece of potato chip.) "Once more. Say pancake."
Robert: "Pancake."
Mother: "Good boy!" (She gives him another potato chip.)

It should be noted that when Robert's mother attempted to bring the words *pan* and *cake* closer and closer together to form the word *pancake,* she did not interrupt this flow with a reward following each of the component parts. Instead, she waited until she got Robert to say the entire word before rewarding his efforts.

It is important to recognize that when children are at the stage of producing two-word combinations, the majority of which consist of single-syllable words, a request for a word that contains three or four syllables represents a more difficult task. Such a single word is, in effect, three or four separate utterances. For example, the word *banana* consists of three distinct syllables: *ba-na-na.* The child may be capable of saying *nana* or *bana* as an approximation of *banana,* but may not be able to string three syllables together to produce the correct pronunciation. As a child becomes fluent with two-word combinations, the additional third syllable is more easily accomplished.

One implication is that the selection of target words for the child who is at the two-word stage should be reviewed to remove words that may contain many more syllables than the child is able to produce at one time. This suggestion does not imply that all three-syllable words should be eliminated from the list, because it is necessary to provide challenges if growth is to occur. Moreover, the child's knowledge of the meanings of words is far more important than articulation when a child is beginning to speak. Thus, two-syllable approximations of three-syllable words should be accepted as reasonable approximations in the beginning. They should be rewarded, and the correct pronunciation should be modeled as Robert's mother did. Words such as *alligator, kangaroo, automobile,* and *umbrella,* which frequently appear in children's picture books, are the kinds of multisyllable words that may present difficulties to children who are learning to string two- or even three-word combinations together. These words should be avoided.

Omitting Initial Consonants

Another common problem is that some children leave off the first sounds of words. For example, they may say *andy* for *candy.* One solution to this problem is to ask your child to repeat several other words he or she can already say that start with the omitted sound. At the end of this sequence of familiar, properly pronounced words, ask your child to say the new word that you are working on. For example, if *candy* is the target word and he or she can say *cup, kiss,* and *car,* you begin by asking your child to say these words before asking for the word *candy.* Next, ask your child to repeat the string of familiar words quickly. Do not interrupt with a reward until the end of the sequence. The repetition of words containing the sound that the child is experiencing difficulty with is one of the more helpful ways to improve articulation.

Omitting Final Sounds

A third type of omission involves leaving off the endings of words—for example, saying *no* rather than *nose*. One solution is to repeat a number of correctly spoken words that rhyme with the misarticulated target word first. Only after repeating the rhyming words that your child knows well, should he or she be asked to say the misarticulated word. If the target word is *hose*, the sequence might go something like this:

Mother:	"Robert, say nose."
Robert:	"Nose."
Mother:	"Say toes."
Robert:	"Toes."
Mother:	"Say rose."
Robert:	"Rose."
Mother:	"Say hose."
Robert:	"Hose." (Mother praises the correct pronunciation of hose and rewards the successful attempt.)

SLURRED SPEECH AND PERSEVERATION

During the early phases of learning to speak, children often slur sounds together or mix them up so that it is sometimes difficult to understand what they are saying. In addition, they may also perseverate, or repeat several times, the particular sound in certain words that they are attempting. They may keep repeating one sound instead of producing all of the different sounds in the word. For example, they may say *baba* for *baby* or *apap* for *apple*. Initially, such approximations or perseverations may be rewarded in an effort to start the child's productive speech. However, in time, you should attempt to correct these articulatory problems. There are at least three useful approaches for dealing with slurred speech and perseverations.

The technique for breaking multisyllable words into smaller parts, described in the section on "Omitting Middle Consonants," can be used to improve slurred and perseverated speech. The procedure for repeating rhyming words that have the same sound as the target word can also be useful to correct slurred speech and the tendency to perseverate. Each of these methods helps your child focus on all of the different sounds necessary to repeat the target word successfully.

A third technique that is often successful is to make the sounds in the word distinct by saying each of them in a different way. For example, you can emphasize the sound that your child is having difficulty with by using a louder voice. If *baby* is the target word and your child persists in saying *baba,* you can emphasize the second syllable by producing it in a louder tone. In other words, say *ba BEE* to your child each time. Still another way to present sounds distinctly is to use a different intonation, or rising and falling pattern of speech, for each part of the word you are teaching. For example, you can let your voice fall off while saying *ba* and then rise while saying *bee.*

CONCLUDING COMMENT

The treatment suggestions above will allow you to elicit correct pronunciations for previously misarticulated words. However, in order for the correct pronunciations to replace the misarticulated ones, it is necessary for you to elicit many repetitions. We suggest having your child say each correctly pronounced word about 60 times each day for several days. Making a game of repeating words and using rewards will help to maintain your child's interest.

Appendix B

NURSERY RHYMES AND SONGS

Children often find it easier and more interesting to drill words if they have the melody of a song or the rhythm of a rhyme to prompt them. Catchy tunes and nursery rhymes with repetitive lyrics are a good technique for producing many repetitions of the same words without becoming excessively boring. A list of appropriate children's songs and nursery rhymes is included below.

Nursery rhymes can serve as an excellent means for involving children in a situation that allows them to become active participants in a "game" that requires words and phrases. Most nursery rhymes consist of short words and easy sounds that are repeated in time to a simple melody. These auditory patterns seem to provide children with clues as to where and when a particular word should be spoken. The fact that they are short and repetitive makes it relatively easy for children to become familiar with both the melody and those words that are part of the repeated phrasing. Songs and nursery rhymes are excellent activities for the teaching sessions.

After you have repeated some of the shorter rhymes for several days, begin to give your child his or her "part." For instance, you can allow your child to "chime in" with the last word to complete each phrase, as in the following rhyme:

Row, row, row your *(boat)*,
Gently down the *(stream)*.
Merrily, merrily,
Merrily, *(merrily)*,
Life is but a *(dream)*.

At first your child may have a one-word part; for example, to say *boat*. However, gradually increase the number of pauses to allow your child to put in his or her word until you are singing a "duet."

148

Be animated and enthusiastic. If your child thinks you are having fun playing this game, he or she is more likely to join in. Pause for 2 or 3 seconds when your child's word is due. If he or she does not say it, you should provide the word and go on to the next part. Encourage your child to join in, and offer praise when he or she does. Verbal praise here is better than food because food and singing are not compatible. Your child's participation with you in the song should be considerably more rewarding than edibles at this point.

We have included just a few of the many familiar songs and nursery rhymes. Others are readily available in children's books, for parents who don't remember or for those who want to expand their singing repertoires.

NURSERY RHYMES

Baa! Baa! Black Sheep
Baa! Baa! Black sheep, have you any wool!
Yes, sir, yes sir, three bags full.
One for my master and one for my dame,
But none for the little boy who cries in the lane.

Hickory, Dickory, Dock
Hickory, dickory, dock,
The mouse ran up the clock.
The clock struck "one," the mouse ran down,
Hickory, dickory, dock.

Humpty Dumpty
Humpty Dumpty sat on a wall,
Humpty Dumpty had a great fall;
All the King's horses and all the King's men,
Couldn't put Humpty together again.

Jack and Jill
Jack and Jill went up the hill,
To fetch a pail of water.
Jack fell down and broke his crown,
And Jill came tumbling after.

Little Bo-Peep
Little Bo-Peep has lost her sheep,
And can't tell where to find them,
Leave them alone, and they'll come home,
Wagging their tails behind them.

Little Jack Horner
Little Jack Horner sat in a corner,
Eating his Christmas pie,
He put in his thumb
And pulled out a plum and said,
"What a good boy am I!"

Mary Had a Little Lamb
Mary had a little lamb,
Its fleece was white as snow.
And everywhere that Mary went,
The lamb was sure to go.

Pat-A-Cake
Pat-a-cake, pat-a-cake, baker's man,
So I will, master, as fast as I can.
Pat it and prick it and mark it with a (T),
And put it in the oven for (Tommy) and me.

Rub-A-Dub-Dub
Rub-a-dub-dub, three men in a tub,
And who d'you think they be?
The butcher, the baker, and candlestick maker,
So turn out the knaves, all three.

This Little Pig Went To Market
This little pig went to market,
This little pig stayed at home,
This little pig had roast beef,
This little pig had none,
And this little pig said, wee, wee, wee,
All the way home.

Three Blind Mice
Three blind mice, three blind mice,
See how they run! See how they run!
They all ran after the farmer's wife,
She cried to the farmer, "Oh save my life!"
The farmer said: "O have no fear, they are nice, the three blind mice.'

Mistress Mary, Quite Contrary
Mistress Mary, quite contrary,
How does your garden grow?
With cockle shells and silver bells,
And pretty maids all in a row.

Hot Cross Buns
Hot cross buns! Hot cross buns!
One a penny, two a penny,
Hot cross buns!
If you have no daughters,
Pray give them to your sons;
But if you have none of these little elves,
Then you must eat them all yourselves.

SONGS

A Tisket, A Tasket
A tisket a tasket, green and yellow basket,
I wrote a letter to my love,
And on the way I dropped it, I dropped it,
And on the way I dropped it.

The Farmer In The Dell

The farmer in the dell,   The farmer takes a wife,
The farmer in the dell,   The farmer takes a wife,
Heigh ho the derry oh,   Heigh ho the derry oh,
The farmer in the dell.   The farmer in the dell.

Old MacDonald Had A Farm
Old MacDonald had a farm, E I E I O!
And on his farm he had some chicks, E I E I O!
With a chick chick here and a chick chick there,
Here a chick, there a chick,
Everywhere a chick chick,
Old MacDonald had a farm, E I E I O!

Pop! Goes The Weasel
All around the cobbler's bench,
The monkey chased the weasel;
The monkey tho't 'twas all in fun,
Pop! Goes the weasel!

Yankee Doodle
Oh, Yankee Doodle came to town, Upon a little pony!
He stuck a feather in his cap, And called it macaroni.
Yankee Doodle doodle do, Yankee Doodle dandy;
All the lads and lassies are as sweet as sugar candy.

Happy Birthday To You
Happy birthday to you,
Happy birthday to you,
Happy birthday dear _____,
Happy birthday to you.

London Bridge
London Bridge is falling down, falling down, falling down,
London Bridge is falling down, My fair lady.

The Mulberry Bush
Here we go round the mulberry bush, The mulberry bush, The
    mulberry bush,
Here we go round the mulberry bush, So early in the morning.

Twinkle, Twinkle, Little Star
Twinkle, twinkle, little star,
How I wonder what you are,
Up above the world so high,
Like a diamond in the sky!
Twinkle, twinkle, little star,
How I wonder what you are.

Rock-A-Bye, Baby
Rock-a-bye, baby, on the tree top,
When the wind blows the cradle will rock;
When the bough breaks the cradle will fall,
And down will come baby, cradle and all.

The ABC Song
A, B, C, D, E, F, G,   Happy, happy shall we be,
H, I, J, K, L, M, N, O, P,   When we've learned our
Q, R, S, and T, U, V,   A, B, C's.
W (double you and) X, Y, Z.

Itsy Bitsy Spider
Itsy bitsy spider, went up the water spout,
Down came the rain and washed the spider out.
Up came the sun and dried out all the rain,
And the itsy bitsy spider went up the spout again.

Index

For Product Safety Concerns and Information please contact our EU
representative GPSR@taylorandfrancis.com
Taylor & Francis Verlag GmbH, Kaufingerstraße 24, 80331 München, Germany

www.ingramcontent.com/pod-product-compliance
Lightning Source LLC
Chambersburg PA
CBHW050524270326
41926CB00015B/3065

9 780805 859461